AMERICAN COUNTRY HOUSES
OF THE GILDED AGE
(Sheldon's "Artistic Country-Seats")

NEW TEXT BY

Arnold Lewis
THE COLLEGE OF WOOSTER
WOOSTER, OHIO

DOVER PUBLICATIONS, INC.
NEW YORK

Copyright © 1982 by Dover Publications, Inc.
All rights reserved under Pan American and International Copyright Conventions.

Published in Canada by General Publishing Company, Ltd., 30 Lesmill Road, Don Mills, Toronto, Ontario.
Published in the United Kingdom by Constable and Company, Ltd.

This Dover edition, first published in 1982, is a republication of all the illustrations from *Artistic Country-Seats: Types of Recent American Villa and Cottage Architecture with Instances of Country Club-Houses*, by George William Sheldon, published by D. Appleton and Co., New York, in 1886–87. An entirely new text has been written for the present edition by Arnold Lewis.

Manufactured in the United States of America
Dover Publications, Inc.
31 East 2nd Street
Mineola, N.Y. 11501

Library of Congress Cataloging in Publication Data
Main entry under title:

American country houses of the Gilded Age (Sheldon's "Artistic country-seats")

Consists primarily of pictorial material from
Artistic country-seats, edited by George William Sheldon
    Bibliography: p.
    1. Country homes—United States—Pictorial works.
2. Country homes—United States—Designs and plans.
3. Architecture, Modern—19th century—United States—Pictorial works.   I. Lewis, Arnold.   II. Sheldon, George William, 1843–1914.   III. Artistic country-seats.
NA7610.A58   728.8'3'0973   81-17384
ISBN 0-486-24301-X (pbk.)   AACR2

PREFACE
AND ACKNOWLEDGMENTS

This volume contains the photographs and plans of the 97 buildings (93 houses and four casinos) that originally appeared in George William Sheldon's *Artistic Country-Seats,* published in 1886–87. It does not, however, include more than samplings of Sheldon's commentaries on the buildings. The original text was extremely long, and often verbose and not directly relevant to the excellent illustations. Instead, new captions have been written for all of the plates. These statements include the most useful information supplied by Sheldon, plus reports about the present condition of each house or casino, analyses of elevations and plans, observations about family life in the 1880s and brief biographical comments about the clients and the architects. Dates, names and locations incorrectly published in *Artistic Country-Seats* have been changed. The last date assigned a building refers to the year in which it was completed. If a date could not be verified, no date was listed. The original order of the photographs has been maintained except for the first five plates. To support the layout requirements of this publication, the Fenn house (formerly plate 5) becomes plate 1, the Osborn house (formerly plates 1 and 2) becomes plates 2 and 3, and the Goelet house (formerly plates 3 and 4) becomes plates 4 and 5.

I needed the assistance of numerous local historians and individuals conversant with late nineteenth-century American architecture to complete this project. Repeatedly, I have been surprised but also grateful and pleased by the willingness of so many to share their insights and knowledge or to search for answers I did not have. I am indebted to all of the following and thank them individually and collectively for their invaluable help:

Miriam Stewart, Fogg Museum, Cambridge, Mass.; Robert Benson, Lawrence Institute of Technology, Southfield, Mich.; Mark Stewart, St. Paul, Minn.; Audrey Wilson, Monmouth College, West Long Branch, N.J.; Richard Longstreth, Kansas State University, Manhattan, Kan.; Ted Sande, Western Reserve Historical Society, Cleveland, O.; David Gebhard, University of California, Santa Barbara, Santa Barbara, Calif.; Davis Erhardt, Queens Borough Public Library, Jamaica, N.Y.; Eric Johannesen, Western Reserve Historical Society, Cleveland, O.; Richard Youngken, Department of Community Development, Glens Falls, N.Y.; J. Earle Stevens, Tuxedo Park, N.Y.; Beatrice Sweeney, Office of the City Historian, Saratoga Springs, N.Y.; Jack Quinan, State University of New York at Buffalo, Buffalo, N.Y.; Carol J. Simms, Gunn Memorial Library, Washington, Conn.; Janet Macomber, Town Historian, New Castle, N.H.; Pamela Schwotzer, Manchester Public Library, Manchester, Mass.; Lucius Wilmerding, Jr., Princeton, N.J.; Gladys O'Neil, Bar Harbor Historical Society, Bar Harbor, Me.; Douglass Tucci, Harvard University, Cambridge, Mass.; Gladys E. Bolhouse, Newport Historical Society, Newport, R.I.; Mark F. Floyd, Germantown Historical Soci-

ety, Philadelphia, Pa.; R. Craig Miller, Metropolitan Museum of Art, New York, N.Y.; Ingrid Meyer, Orange Public Library, Orange, N.J.; George Moss, Seabright, N.J.; Mary McTamaney, Tuxedo Park Library, Tuxedo Park, N.Y.; Eleanor M. Price, Upper Montclair, N.J.; Lucy Fitzgerald, Montclair Public Library, Montclair, N.J.; Margaret Floyd, Tufts University, Medford, Mass.; Roger Lewis, Bower-Lewis-Thrower, Architects, Philadelphia, Pa.; Alma Gay Fowler, Stratford Historical Society, Stratford, Conn.; Perry G. Fisher, Columbia Historical Society, Washington, D.C.; Joan Plungis, Cincinnati Historical Society, Cincinnati, O.; Helen Login, Public Library, Millburn, N.J.; R. James Tobin, Boston College, Chestnut Hill, Mass.; Beth Rich, Needham Free Public Library, Needham Heights, Mass.; Marion Nicholson, Greenwich Library, Greenwich, Conn.; Jean N. Berry, Wellesley Historical Society, Wellesley, Mass.; Arthur J. Gerrier, Maine Historical Society, Portland, Me.; Robert R. Perron, Beverly Historical Society, Beverly, Mass.; Katharine H. Winslow, Narragansett Pier Free Library, Narragansett, R.I.; Carol Woodger, Port Chester Public Library, Port Chester, N.Y.; Catherine Harper, Plainfield Public Library, Plainfield, N.J.; Bruce Cole, Crandall Library, Glens Falls, N.Y.; Jacqueline Bearden, Saint Augustine Historical Society, Saint Augustine, Fl.; J. Robert Starkey, East Orange Public Library, East Orange, N.J.; Margarett M. Kennard, Lenox Library, Lenox, Mass.; Frances Burnett, Manchester, Mass.; Tom Martinson, Ellerbe Associates, Inc., Bloomington, Minn.; Richard Tyler, Philadelphia Historical Commission, Philadelphia, Pa.

For their reliable and conscientious assistance with the manuscript, I thank Evelyn Blake, Bettye Jo Riebe, Lee Ann Davisson and Doug Goodwin.

I am grateful to Steven McQuillin for reading all of my commentaries and for reminding me persistently that we should accept and value architecture regardless of whether it clings to the past or anticipates the future.

I thank Beth Irwin Lewis for her constant encouragement, perceptive insights, pertinent criticism and wise recommendations and Martha Lewis for discovering that 40 of the photographs in the original publication were printed reversed. I am most grateful to my fine editor, James Spero, for providing readers with a clearer text to read. I have appreciated the creative suggestions of Clarence Strowbridge of Dover, who understood the need for this inexpensive reprint and who recommended combining nineteenth-century illustrations with twentieth-century research.

Finally, I thank The College of Wooster, that admirable institution where I have been fortunate to teach, for its confidence in me expressed through its faculty development program and through a grant from The Henry Luce III Fund for Distinguished Scholarship.

Wooster, Ohio June, 1981   A. L.

SHELDON
AND *ARTISTIC COUNTRY-SEATS*

In his brief prefatory note to *Artistic Country-Seats* (1886–87), George William Sheldon wrote that architects had made a significant contribution to the "Renaissance of American art," a development inspired by the Centennial Exposition of 1876, and that their achievements could be seen most clearly in the "country-seat." Consequently, his purpose in preparing the portfolio was "to present, in as direct and attractive a form as possible, an exposition of this triumph." Subtitled *Types of Recent American Villa and Cottage Architecture with Instances of Country Club-Houses,* and arranged in two volumes with five parts, it was published in 500 copies by D. Appleton and Co. of New York for those who had subscribed to the project. The first volume contained 50 exterior photographs and 47 first-floor plans of 44 different houses and three casinos; the second volume contained 50 photographs and plans of 49 different houses and one casino. Sheldon wrote commentaries for each of the 97 executed buildings, some as short as two pages in length, some as long as six. The text of the first volume consisted of 220 pages and that of the second, 187.

These photographs and informative plans are evidence of the craftsmanship of builders, the creative design, practical planning and technological receptivity of architects, and the confidence and adequate bank accounts of clients in the period from 1878 to 1887. Vincent Scully, who drew heavily upon Sheldon in his masterful and often-cited study, *The Shingle Style* (1955), claimed that *Artistic Country-Seats* and *Artistic Houses,* which Sheldon prepared for Appleton in 1883–84, were the two most important contemporaneous sources for understanding the shingle style.[1]

Sheldon was born on January 28, 1843 in Summerville, S.C., the first son of the Rev. George and Martha Lyman Sheldon. After graduating from Princeton with a bachelor's degree in 1863, he tutored there in Latin and belles lettres while studying for his master's degree from 1865 to 1867. He then joined the faculty of Union Theological Seminary where he remained as instructor in Oriental languages until 1873. For several years he worked as the art critic for the New York *Evening Post* and from 1890 until 1900 was literary adviser in London for D. Appleton and Co. He died in Summit, N.J. on January 29, 1914.

From the late 1870s until he moved to London, Sheldon published frequently with Appleton and Co., particularly on recent American art. In 1879 *American Painters* appeared, 50 biographical and critical essays on known and obscure artists; in 1882 *Hours with Art and Artists,* chatty and casual commentaries on contemporary artists in France, Britain and the United States; in 1883–84 *Artistic Houses,* 203 fine photographs and descriptions of the country's costliest interiors; in 1885–86 *Selections in Modern Art;* in 1888 *Recent Ideals of American Art,* copperplate reproductions of 184 oil and wa-

tercolor paintings; and in 1890 *Ideals of Life in France* and *Women in French Art,* each consisting of 225 plates of paintings and drawings. He also wrote for the leading art periodicals of the day. For example, in 1880 he published one of the first positive assessments of Winslow Homer's "American shepherdess" type for the *Art Journal* (April), and for *Harper's Monthly* (February) "A Symposium of Wood-Engravers," today regarded as one of the most valuable commentaries on this medium written during its late nineteenth-century revival. However, he was probably more versatile and prolific as a writer than authoritative; in 1882 he published a 575-page account of the volunteer fire department of New York City and two years later *Harper's* carried his article on the "Old Packet and Clipper Service."

Collecting Materials

Information about the process Sheldon used to produce *Artistic Country-Seats* is scant today. Judging from his statements about the individual houses and casinos, he visited some but not all of them. Many of his commentaries are thorough, confident and informed, suggesting that he was writing from personal notes. Describing the parlor of the Wood house (plate 10), he wrote, "It has no wainscoting, but the mantel is very beautiful, its lower part having two square fluted columns supporting the shelf, which are continued to the cornice, inclosing a circular mirror of beveled glass, with carved spandrels, and five small square mirrors of beveled glass on each side of it."[2] Other descriptions, however, lack such intimate familiarity with decorative or constructive detail. The general observations and statistical information that characterize many of his statements may indicate that he was dependent on the photograph and plan or on material supplied by client or architect.

In reference to the Howard house (plate 51), he explained that "the ground plan, given below—for which we are indebted to the architect—is drawn from a point of view different from that chosen by the photographer."[3] In all probability, he relied on the architects for the plans and did not take the pictures himself. The quality of the photographs is so good for this period that professionals must have been responsible. The Gutekunst Co. of Philadelphia, founded by Frederick Gutekunst (1831–1917), claimed in an advertisement that it was responsible for the photographic work of both *Artistic Houses* and *Artistic Country-Seats.*[4] Did this mean clicking the camera as well as producing the photogelatine prints, or only the latter? While this is unclear, there is some evidence suggesting that this anthology was the work of a single photographer.

The clarity of the plates is unusually high and consistent. The photograph of the Geiger house (plate 9) is one of the rare examples of a slightly unfocused shot. Furthermore, the set represents competent architectural photography: well-composed pictures which, despite challenges of length (plate 92) or rambling plan (plate 39), seldom slice off the ends of a principal facade. Roofs are not washed out by the light of the sky above, and references to the environment do not interfere with an examination of the house. Though trees abound on these properties, only infrequently do they obstruct our study of the elevations (plates 46, 51, 71 and 86). Another reason for concluding that one person might have been responsible for these photographs is the perspective from which the shot was taken. In 80 percent of the houses the view is angled and either mildly left or mildly right of center, a position from which the principal facade could be studied easily and a secondary facade less effectively. For some small, square houses, the camera emphasized the relative equality of two facades, as in the J. H. Smith house (plate 41), the Hemenway house (plate 49) and the Mallory house (plate 50). The third and least frequent position was on the perpendicular, which divided the composition into two balanced parts. This can be seen in the photographs of the Cook residence (plate 14) and the Scott residence (plate 69).

These photographs are surprisingly similar in several other ways. When the terrain permitted, the photographer or photographers called attention to the surroundings, particularly to the luxurious flat lawns, the graceful sweep of driveways, or paths leading to steps and porches. Perhaps the most consistent feature and certainly the least expected is the absence of signs that red-blooded American families lived in these cottages and villas. Except in a few photographs (plates 10, 34, 45, 60, 61 and 91), people are not to be seen on these premises or even standing behind windows. We must be content with reminders that humans have been or will be there—a chair left in the front yard of the Netter house (plate 57), the open windows of the Newcomb (plate 76) and several other houses, or the nets anticipating or recalling games played on the casino lawn at Elberon (plate 78). Where are all the horses and carriages for whom these drives and porte-cocheres were built? Even signs of construction, junk or unfinished plantings are difficult to find. Strangely, these houses look isolated, naked, empty, silent despite their beautiful surroundings and animated designs; the Cook house (plate 14) is a case in point. Of course some of these houses were empty because they were used for only few months during the year and many of the photographs were taken when the summer or mountain season had ended. Also, Sheldon's anthology was so contemporary that several families had not yet moved in.

On the other side, it can be argued that more than one photographer was involved because the distance from which the photographs were taken varies considerably. The Josephs (plate 11), Gibson (plate 20), Howard (plate 51) and Washburn (plate 72) houses were photographed from vantage points that made their form take precedence over their detail. Given the size of these four, this may seem to be an inevitable result, but two of the largest residences in the Philadelphia suburbs, the houses for E. N. Benson (plate 40) and H. H. Houston (plate 70), were photographed at much closer range. In several instances of spectacular photography, the close range enhances the detail to the detriment of the form and confronts the viewer with the physical presence of the materials. Though modest in size, the French house (plate 6), the Hemenway cottage (plate 49) and the Van Buren retreat in Tuxedo Park (plate 61) make aggressive visual demands on us that are unexpectedly modern in their anticipation of the motion picture's fascination with detail and the Pop artist's penchant for disquieting scale.

Assuming that the dates for the completion of these cottages and villas are reasonably accurate, the photographs were probably taken between the summer of 1885 and the summer of 1886. The growth of plant life, particularly ivy, around some of the older houses, such as the Vanderbilt residence (plate 33) of 1877–78 or the Netter house (plate 57) of 1881, reinforces this conclusion. It is impossible to reconstruct the itinerary of the photographer or photographers. Although the houses at Newport appear to have been recorded in summer or later summer, two of the houses at Lenox-Stockbridge were caught in winter and two during the summer months.

The plans of these houses and casinos were probably sent by the architects to Sheldon. Then each of the major rooms of the first floor of these buildings was identified in the same typeface, the Geiger plan (plate 9), probably labeled by the architect, being an exception. The size of these plans was determined by the size of the page and not by the dimensions of the house. The plans of the Dod house (plate 34) and the Noakes house (plate 77) are drafted in a distinctive style, but most of the others, in part because of the similarity in size and identifying type, suggest, at first glance, similar drafting signatures. On second glance, however, variations become evident. These can be detected in the hand printing marking small spaces (such as plates 12, 42 and 76), the decision to include or exclude references to door openings (plate 72), the direction of stairways (plates 60 and 97), ceiling ribs (plate 1) or floor patterns (plate 94), and the various stylistic means for identifying porch columns (plates 7 and 81) or even a window.

Dates of Construction, Locations and Architects

Sheldon's survey of country houses and country clubs was decidedly up-to-date. Seven of the buildings have not been dated because verifying information was lacking. The date or dates given the remaining 90 buildings refer to the year in which the construction was completed. Of these 90 houses or casinos, two were built in 1878–79, ten in 1880–81, 22 in 1882–83, 33 in 1884–85 and 23 in 1886–87. This means that 62 percent of the dated buildings were completed in 1884 or later.

Sheldon found these examples of his new American Renaissance primarily in New England and the Middle Atlantic states. Only 18 of the houses were located outside of these two regions, and these tended to be principal homes of families living in or near major cities (Cleveland, Cincinnati, Chicago, Detroit and St. Paul–Minneapolis) rather than second or third-house country seats. The houses located in the suburbs of major cities tended to be somewhat larger and were usually constructed of brick or stone while those along the coast or in the mountains tended to be smaller and were often built of wood. However, there are numerous exceptions to both of these generalizations. Over one-third of the examples were erected in three areas—

Newport-Narragansett Pier, the suburbs of Philadelphia and the metropolitan suburbs of northern New Jersey. In the order of the number of houses and clubs included in *Artistic Country-Seats*, the cities and regions are:

Newport-Narragansett Pier, R.I.	13
Philadelphia and its suburbs, Pa.	12
Northern New Jersey	11
Long Branch coast, N.J.	7
Boston suburbs, Mass.	6
St. Paul-Minneapolis, Minn.	6
Tuxedo Park, N.Y.	5
Cleveland, Ohio	5
Lenox-Stockbridge, Mass.	4
Manchester-by-the-Sea, Mass.	4
Cincinnati, Ohio	3
Far Rockaway—Lawrence, N.Y.	2
Buffalo, N.Y.	2
Bar Harbor and Mt. Desert, Me.	2
Greenwich-Bryam, Conn.	2
Saratoga Springs, N.Y.	2
Chicago, Ill.	1
Falmouth Foreside, Me.	1
Glens Falls, N.Y.	1
Grosse Pointe Farms, Mich.	1
Mamaroneck, N.Y.	1
New Castle, N.H.	1
New York, N.Y.	1
St. Augustine, Fla.	1
Stratford, Conn.	1
Washington, Conn.	1
Washington, D.C.	1

Although the buildings included in *Artistic Country-Seats* were designed by 47 different architects, two-thirds of them were done by 17 firms. The prestigious and very busy firm of McKim, Mead & White was responsible for one-sixth of the examples that Sheldon selected. He clearly recognized the spatial and compositional changes occurring in the design and planning of American frame houses in the first half of the 1880s and included many of the firms responsible for what Scully has termed "the shingle style." That Scully reproduced 33 photographs from this collection is a tribute to Sheldon's ability to pinpoint a significant trend against the confusing and architecturally eclectic background of this decade. Furthermore, Sheldon called attention to designers who present-day historians and critics, aided by decades of perspective, have concluded were among the genuine innovators of the period, such individuals and firms as McKim, Mead & White; Bruce Price; Lamb and Rich; W. R. Emerson; Peabody and Stearns; Clarence Luce; Arthur Little; Henry Richardson; Wilson Eyre, Jr.; and J. C. Stevens. On the other hand, Sheldon was open-minded, for he also included in his anthology costly and enormous structures built of durable materials and designed in revival styles. To call him open-minded may be a polite way of saying that he had an underdeveloped idea of what domestic architecture in the 1880s should be. He could praise with apparently equal fervor and sincerity designs stripped of the pulse and risks inherent in those cottages of wood, pretentious and heavy aca-

demic machines that announced so clearly the frantic search of new wealth for historical and cultural trappings. Since this series was "printed for the subscribers" and since some of these subscribers were probably the owners of the houses illustrated, he might also be accused of having the backbone of a chocolate éclair.

Consequently, his designation "country-seat" is not very narrow or precise. For Sheldon, it embraced large and small, cheap and expensive, structures built of a variety of materials, located in the heart of cities or in remote regions and used either for a few months of the year or uninterruptedly as the family's sole residence. Yet this publication is an extremely valuable document of the period. If twentieth-century historians have slighted the diversity and pedestrian or reactionary expressions of this decade, Sheldon celebrated its pluralism and respected its products. As a result, his story of the domestic architecture of the 1880s is told with a different and larger cast of characters than the ones we usually hear. We learn, for example, of the influence of Theophilus P. Chandler, Jr., in the suburbs of Philadelphia, of Clarence Johnston in St. Paul and of W. Halsey Wood in East Orange, N.J.

The firms that designed more than one building illustrated in *Artistic Country-Seats*, and the number of their works included, are:

McKim, Mead & White	16
Bruce Price	8
Peabody and Stearns	5
Theophilus P. Chandler, Jr.	4
Lamb and Rich	4
Willcox and Johnston	3
Arthur B. Jennings	3
Wilson Eyre, Jr.	3
Addison Hutton	3
Charles F. Schweinfurth	3
W. Halsey Wood	3
William R. Emerson	2
G. W. and W. D. Hewitt	2
Clarence S. Luce	2
Arthur Little	2
James McLaughlin	2
Edmund M. Wheelwright	2

The firms responsible for only one house each are Allen and Kenway, William B. Bigelow, A. Page Brown, Cobb and Frost, Arthur H. Dodd, H. Edwards Ficken, Robert W. Gibson, Green and Wicks, Charles C. Haight, Francis H. Kimball, Long and Kees, James B. Lord, Mason and Rice, E. Townsend Mix, George T. Pearson, William A. Potter, Henry H. Richardson, Rossiter and Wright, Rotch and Tilden, Julius Schweinfurth, S. Gifford Slocum, Charles H. Smith, Franklin W. Smith, George Smith, Douglas Smythe, John C. Stevens, Sturgis and Brigham, Van Campen Taylor, C. Howard Walker, and George Wirth.

Financial Clout of the Owners

In his comments on these photographs and plans Sheldon contended that the "new" American architect understood that well-designed houses did not require large amounts of money.

He has shown by demonstration that a simple, effective, comfortable, and artistic cottage may be erected for, say four thousand dollars, which shall produce upon the spectator precisely the influence of a piece of Greek statuary or a theme of classic music; that, in a word, the effect of beauty is not dependent upon quantity; and that in little things, in modest dwellings, as well as in more ostentatious abodes, the beauty that is a joy forever may have a local habitation and a name.[5]

To illustrate this point, he included a few houses that evidently had been built for less than $10,000 (plates 9, 41, 95), houses that were usually small and constructed largely but not necessarily exclusively of wood. The average house in this collection, however, was built for much more than $10,000, and despite his pleas for modesty, Sheldon was obviously pleased with several that cost ten and even 20 times as much. Determining the cost of these houses is difficult because we often do not know what the available figure entails, whether it refers only to the design and construction or also to the costs of interior decoration and landscaping. Even though the following figures may be somewhat debatable, they provide a general guide for understanding the monetary value of the houses that Sheldon included in *Artistic Country-Seats*. The costs of 62—58 houses and four casinos—of the total of 97 buildings are known. For the 58 houses, the categories and number of houses in each category are:

under $10,000	5
$10,000–$20,000	17
$20,000–$30,000	11
$30,000–$40,000	4
$40,000–$50,000	5
$50,000–$60,000	2
$60,000–$70,000	2
$70,000–$80,000	2
$80,000–$90,000	3
$90,000–$100,000	1
$100,000–$150,000	3
$150,000–$200,000	1
over $200,000	2

The two residences valued at more than $200,000 were the Everett house (plate 47), $225,000, and the Washburn house (plate 72), $250,000. It is conceivable that several of the houses for which no figures are readily available could have cost $100,000 or more—Gibson (plate 20), Taylor (plate 37), Benson (plate 40), Palmer (plate 45), Milbank (plate 68) and Brush (plate 73). The costs of the four casinos were: Newport (plates 16 and 17), $64,000; Short Hills (plate 26), $9,000; Narrangansett Pier (plate 52), $66,480; and Elberon (plate 78), $17,725.

Although the professions or businesses of 77 of the 93 house owners have been identified, it is impossible to create an efficient and reliable list of work categories because many of them (J. W. Johnson, Henry H. Houston, Chauncey W. Griggs and Sylvester T. Everett, for example) were often active at a given time in more than one business venture. Houston tried his magic touch on railroads, lake steamers, ocean vessels, oil, gold mines in the West and real estate in Philadelphia's 22nd ward. Those active in education, the ministry or law are much easier to categorize, but they represent a very small proportion of the total number, a figure unquestionably dominated by individuals who earned their money in banking or finance, trade, manufacturing or commercial enterprises. For the following list each home owner was assigned a principal occupation even though several men could be associated with more than one.

banking and finance	12
merchandising	11
manufacturing	9
Lumber	6
trade	6
publishing and printing	5
creative art	4
law	4
railroads	4
real estate	3
tobacco	3
construction	2
military	2
utilities	2
education	1
government service	1
medicine	1
ministry	1

These "cottages" and "country-seats" were made possible by the optimism and self-confidence of both clients and architects, by available land usually obtainable at reasonable rates, by the possibility and desire for leisure time, by the growing reaction to the city as a place for raising families and, above all, by an expanding economy that made quick fortunes easy and their public demonstrations irresistible. Though we cannot estimate the collective worth of those who owned the houses in this collection, it is safe to say that such a figure would be difficult to comprehend today.

Millionaires were not scarce on Sheldon's roster. Some names are easily recognized, the Vanderbilts or the Lorillards, for example, but most of us in the 1980s are unaware that H. A. C. Taylor's father, Moses, left $40,000,000 at his death in 1882, that Jeremiah Milbank left an estate valued at $32,000,000 in 1884, and that Mary Hemenway and her children inherited $20,000,000 in 1876. The families included in *Artistic Country-Seats* had money to spend, and they spent it freely on architecture, decoration and property. The Washburn estate (plate 72) in Minneapolis, laid out by F. L. Olmsted, was estimated in the mid-1880s to be worth three-quarters of a million dollars. $20,000 were spent on the plumbing of the main house alone. The barn of the Johnson house (plate 66), also in Minneapolis, was constructed of Kasota stone for $15,000. William Weld paid $40,000 for his stable and christened it with one of Boston's most expensive barn parties of the 1880s. William D. Sloane's retreat (plate 94) at Lenox, Mass. contained 13 bedrooms for servants. The grounds of Louis Lorillard's "cottage" at Newport required six gardeners. Henry C. Gibson's 210-foot long "Maybrook" was less than ten miles from his principal residence on Walnut Street in Philadelphia. He needed the walls of both houses to hang his extensive collection of paintings. The $100,000 Kidder house (plate 92), which the photographer probably thought would never end, was one of three houses the family owned in and around Boston. Pierre Lorillard once said, "A man with a hundred thousand a year is in the unhappy position where he can see what a good time he could have if he only had the money." Many of the owners of these houses had Lorillard's kind of money, and one way they had a good time was to use architecture to show it off.

Outside, the wealth of the family could be conveyed by the spaciousness and landscaping of the grounds, the dimensions of the building and the style and materials in which it was erected. Inside, this wealth was usually conveyed by the elegance and cultural messages of the interior decoration. Sheldon's descriptions are often model demonstrations of how these interiors were meant to be appreciated. The following is a portion of his description of Louis Lorillard's cottage at Newport (plate 100):

Of unusual beauty is the piano-case of Canima-wood, decorated with painted figures and flowers by Cottier and Company, at a cost of three thousand dollars. Cabinets, tables, and chairs are all of the same Canima-wood, and all resplendent with the traces of the painters's brush and the gilder's tool.

The feature of Mr. Lorillard's dining-room is the deep canvas frieze, on which Mr. Walter Crane has painted a series of figure-pieces delineating the story of Longfellow's "Skeleton in Armor," with a success that has caused it to be described and reproduced in art journals and newspapers on each side of the water. The high wainscot is in oak, in small panels, and the mantel is a singularly fine piece of delicate carving. The Gothic chairs of oak, covered with morocco, are English in style.

The hall has a ceiling of deep-beamed oak, and high wainscot of the same wood, and all the wall-spaces are hung with Flemish tapestries. Its magnificent stained-glass window, on the first landing of the staircase, contains life-size, brilliant figures from the old Norse mythology, by William Morris and Burne-Jones.[6]

Unlike many architectural historians who gloss over or avoid interior decoration, Sheldon considered the finish and presentation of the interior as an integral and important part of architecture, drew constantly on his knowledge of painting, sculpture and the decorative arts, and thoroughly enjoyed writing about these issues.

Record of Preservation

Despite the fine glass, rare woods, and prized stone, let alone the effort and the pride of client, builder and designer, the majority of the buildings in this series have been destroyed, accidentally or intentionally. We do not value or respect history, regardless of our sweet clichés to the contrary. Our decisions affecting the products of history are usually made primarily on the basis of the self-interest of the present. Consequently, yesterday's triumphs and proud accomplishments often become today's burdens and obstacles. Only 38 of these houses and casinos remain, several of them so altered that they would not be recognized today (plates 60 and 76, for example).

In this series the houses least likely to survive were those built within the limits of one of the large cities of the Eastern seaboard or the Midwest. All of the ones in these photographs erected in New York, Washington, D.C., Cleveland, Cincinnati, Chicago and Minneapolis have been destroyed. They were removed primarily for two reasons: the value of the property on which they stood increased significantly, and they were too large for families of subsequent generations to maintain. St. Paul and Philadelphia are two exceptions to this urban destruction. Three of the four residences built on Summit Avenue in St. Paul (plates 44, 46,

48) and two of the seven within Philadelphia (plates 12 and 70) are extant. If a residence was erected in the suburbs of a large city instead of within the city, its chances of survival were somewhat better. Detroit's only suburban house is gone, as are four of the six built around Boston, eight of the 11 erected in the New York metropolitan area of New Jersey, and three of the five in the communities west of Philadelphia.

There is no consistent survival pattern for those built at coastal or inland resorts. Preservationists in Newport-Narragansett Pier have been distinctly more successful than anywhere else; nine of 13 remain. On the other hand, Bar Harbor-Mt. Desert has lost its two houses, Manchester-by-the-Sea two of four and the Long Branch region five of seven, while, inland, Tuxedo Park has lost three of five, Lenox-Stockbridge two of four and Saratoga Springs both of its structures.

Records often do not indicate why a house or casino was removed. Based on available information, most of the structures in *Artistic Country-Seats* that are not extant were intentionally razed. Charles F. Brush even specified that his house (plate 73) was to be torn down after his death. The second most frequent cause of destruction has been fire. Mt. Desert's devastating fire of 1947 took the Howard cottage (plate 51) and an earlier blaze destroyed "Chatwold" (plate 31). Like "Chatwold," several buildings consumed in spectacular fires were not of wood but of less combustible materials (plates 85 and 96, for example). Wooden structures, however, have been understandably more vulnerable to flame, as Cornelius Vanderbilt (plate 33) and Spencer Trask (plate 93) discovered. Part of the Newport Casino (plates 16 and 17) has been burned, as has the wooden section of the Narragansett Pier Casino (plate 52) and all of the Short Hills Casino (plate 26). The receding shoreline at Monmouth Beach north of Long Branch has eliminated the Herter house (plate 18) and George F. Baker's cottage (plate 19). Major alterations have been undertaken for obvious reasons such as structural deterioration or the need for more room (plates 36 and 41). Changes in taste have also been responsible for drastic face-lifts. The shingle-style houses, in particular, have been transformed because later generations have often been embarrassed by their stimulating texture and asymmetrical and spatially expressive compositions. The Newcomb cottage (plate 76) is a case in point.

Sheldon's Stated and Implied Attitudes

In addition to containing considerable factual information about the exteriors and interiors of these houses, Sheldon's commentaries also revealed his optimism about the United States, his assumption about the life-style and privileges of the families who owned these buildings and his pleasure over the increasing stature of the architects who designed them.

Sheldon was delighted to be an American in the mid-1880s. He thought the future of the country was unthreatened and the opportunities available to its people unlimited. He thought the progress of the future would be even more impressive than the progress of the past. How stunned he would have been in 1886 had he known that the Leech house (plate 99) in Saratoga Springs, so "stately without and convenient within," would be unoccupied 11 years after it was completed. Sheldon, unaffected as we are today by concerns about the limits of resources, assumed that there was as much space available in the United States as good money could buy and enough organic and inorganic materials to satisfy the domestic desires of anyone who wanted to build. To him, the family that purchased 50 acres of land to protect its summer cottage was not greedily appropriating land that others might share, but artistically developing the American landscape. Furthermore, he did not object if the owners erected a cottage large enough for ten families to live in simultaneously, and he did not raise questions if a family used its miniature hotel for only a fraction of the year.

Undisturbed by the taking of space, Sheldon was also undisturbed by the consumption of materials. To the contrary, he was impressed by quantity. He considered the unrestrained expenditures on so many of these houses a sign of the vitality of American architecture. He liked to describe interiors crammed with fine woods, glass and silks from around the world. His accounts are filled with respectful acknowledgments of woodwork in Santo Domingo mahogany, Hungarian ash or California redwood, of walls decorated with tapestries from Flanders or papers and silks from Japan, of fireplaces finished in English sandstone and Siena marble, of Moorish screenwork, of Renaissance ironwork, of beveled glass mirrors from France, of Dutch and German tiles, and the like. Sheldon was more taken by the accumulation and inclusion of these fine materials and precious objects than by the quality of their presentation. If owner, architect and interior designer did not know when to stop, he never objected.

He admired these clients because they had been successful in the competitive marketplace or had made it in the courts or the universities. With the majority of those of his background and training, he subscribed to the notion that individuals who had earned wealth were entitled to display it. To use architecture as display was not only a material way of proving the recent prosperity of the United States but an act of faith in the continuation of the conditions that caused this prosperity.

Sheldon also endorsed the right of these owners to separate themselves from other people, to spend their leisure time away from the city and its increasing crowdedness, anonymity and confusion. These houses prove that they retreated to the suburbs, the mountains or the seaside, either to live for periods of the year in peace and isolation or to live close to individuals of like breeding, outlook and means. In 1885 and 1886 Pierre Lorillard closely controlled the matter of who could live in Tuxedo Park and who could not. Because so many eminent families with time on their hands settled at Tuxedo, Newport, Lenox, Manchester-by-the-Sea, Elberon—the list of such social communities is long—visiting and being visited became major events of each day, and both architects and those who laid out the grounds paid much attention to coming and going.

Despite the flexible planning of most of these houses and their pleasant locations at the seaside, in the mountains or even in the suburbs, Sheldon's constant reminders—the figures after della Robbia, the elegance of a dining room, the imported woodwork—warn us not to assume that informality characterized vacation life. Certainly, life at the country seat was more relaxed than in the city, but it was also much more proper than we might expect. This becomes clear when reading these descriptions. Although Sheldon tried, when information was available, to comment on numerous spaces and functions within a house, sometimes even reporting on the equipment in the basement or explaining the subdivisions of the attic, the rooms that repeatedly attracted his attention and held his interest were the reception room, hall, parlor and dining room. These were the social spaces where the family had spent its money on interior decoration and where, in effect, it was on display. Most of these families while at the country seat maintained a heavy schedule of entertaining. Perhaps Sheldon did not mean to stress the importance of public display to the extent he did. Perhaps his assumption of its importance is not wholly valid. Nevertheless, his descriptions and his choices of houses leave the impression that despite the more casual ways of the shore or the countryside, the important moments of life within were to be conducted properly and formally.

These houses were not planned and finished to serve all members of the family equally. They were created to meet the needs of the master and the mistress. References to children are difficult to find on these plans, and Sheldon ignores their existence entirely. The servants, the third group that lived in these summer homes, were also well hidden. Architects labored to make sure that servants could support the activities of the house without interfering with those who were engaged in them. From the outside the areas in which they worked and slept were de-emphasized as far as possible without harming the unity of the design.

The "New" American Architect

Sheldon argued that during the first half of the 1880s American architects became more confident, paid less attention to historical styles than their teachers had, and were creating distinctive forms that signified the emergence of "a native style of architecture." Already, the country house, that type which "represents his triumphs much better and more generally than do his designs in any other sphere of effort," had "won the admiration of Europe."[7] In fact, claimed Sheldon, France's superiority in the design of country houses was now in doubt. Furthermore, the quality of the American country house would improve because its architects were in tune with their times.

For, taking him in his most characteristic and creditable manifestations, he is as truly an artist as any other architect that ever lived. If the architect of the Parthenon deserves consideration because he was the true son of his era, giving to the world a noble expression of himself under the conditions of his environment, . . in like manner the architect of the representative American country-seat, in the last quarter of the nineteenth century, may be styled a true son of his epoch, giving to the world a noble expression of himself under the conditions of his environment. At Newport, at Elberon, Manchester-by-the-Sea, in the suburbs of Chicago, Cleveland, Boston, New York, Philadelphia, San Francisco, and St. Augustine, he has erected monuments alike of his age and of his genius.[8]

This passage contains several stylistic traits found throughout Sheldon's text: expansive generalizations, fine-sounding but unclear phrases like "true son" and "noble expression," and the tendency to speak of "conditions of his environment" instead of pointing out what those conditions were. The passage also makes clear his attempt to convince readers of the new stature of American architects. Sheldon played the role of an educator, one who discovered talent and then tried to convince the American public to respect these designers, primarily by treating them as professionals and listening to them. "To-day the architect is universally recognized an an artist, and is never confounded with the mechanic."[9] To illustrate the architects' new position of authority, he told of being in the offices of McKim, Mead & White when the interior decorator for their Villard house, New York City (1883), arrived.

Such an incident, in which a well-known and prosperous house-decorator appears in the studio of the architect and waits to receive instructions, is one of the most significant signs of the times, and, to the architect, one of the most hopeful.[10]

The subordination of the decorator was, in part, the result of the architect's desire to exert greater influence.

Belonging to the new epoch, he must necessarily be *au fond* an artist; as an artist he can not build a house to advantage without the opportunity of considering it as an *ensemble*, and adapting every detail both of external form and internal ornament to its inherent needs.[11]

Specifically, this meant

the American architect of the present epoch desires to be his own landscape gardener, and for precisely the same reasons that he desires to be his own house-decorator. He views the arrangement of the grounds around the structure as part of the whole effect which he is striving to create.[12]

Sheldon contended that there was a new though unwritten book of etiquette covering the client's role: "the influence of the architect upon his client has increased in direct ratio with the progress of the new epoch in which we are living; and that to-day a person who wants a house built has less disposition to dictate to his architect on questions of taste than he had five years ago."[13] He envisioned the architect, then, not only as a designer of fine houses but also as an essential instructor in public taste. In the Middle Ages, explained Sheldon, clients knew what they wanted and "knew a beautiful thing when they saw it"; consequently, the architect listened to them. In the 1880s the taste of clients was not as well developed and their objectives less clearly defined. Until American taste matured, the burden of knowing and explaining "the beautiful" would fall on the architect. If this taste did not develop, the future of architecture in the United States would be clouded.

In Sheldon's opinion, the advantage American architects had over their counterparts in Europe was their greater freedom to disregard the influence of historical styles and schools of Western architecture. "It has been said that in America we have no inheritance of ruins and no embarrassments of tradition, and are free from historical prejudice; that we are therefore in a position to appreciate earnest and honest effort..."[14] Two factors encouraged this freedom. The issues of time and distance were the first; the United States had not existed during the Renaissance or Medieval periods and thus could not have genuine monu-

ments of these periods on its soil. The second was the growing confidence of these designers, which inspired increasingly independent thinking. Sheldon's conclusions paralleled those of some critics in Britain, France and Germany in the mid-1880s who contended that the "chains" of the grand tradition of architecture did not shackle the Americans to the extent they seemed to restrict architects in Europe.

The Question of Style

Because the grip of the grand tradition was looser, the architects of the United States could exploit this tradition more easily. One result was buildings created from more than one stylistic source. Referring to the Scott house (plate 69) by George Pearson, Sheldon wrote:

So far as style is concerned, the building can not be classified; and in this respect it is practically like most of the structures represented in this collection. But Mr. Pearson does not assume that non-compliance with any set style necessarily deprives a dwelling of features on which the artistic imagination may be worthily exerted, and in which new ideas may be brought into place. The value of the result depends upon the freedom of the architect within the range of the vitalizing ideas of his art.[15]

Lighter obligations to the past and more flexible utilization of any historical system of architecture, coupled with increasing self-confidence, produced variety, "and the great variety of development which characterizes the present Renaissance of American architecture, as exemplified in this portfolio, is, to our mind, one of the most wholesome signs of promise."[16]

The term Sheldon chose to express this variety was "eclectic." In his discussion of the Brown house (plate 38), he gave the fullest statement of what he meant by this.

Undoubtedly the finest results of the present Renaissance of American architecture, as applied to country-seats, have been obtained by disciples of the eclectic school—men who, having a just sense of the conditions of each particular case that comes within their view, feel themselves free to use any means or methods that are adapted to secure the desired end. Without special preferences, without special apostleship, they have survived the products of the architect from China to Peru; they have become conversant with the best that has been thought and done in architecture; and they have drawn upon their resources in all directions in perfecting each individual plan. To them, the Classicists are mere copyists; the Gothic votaries are mere copyists; the men of the Italian and French Renaissance are mere copyists. They propose to exercise the untrammeled freedom of the artist of the nineteenth century; they are determined to enter into the liberty with which the nineteenth century has made them free...[17]

Vincent Scully was the first to point out Sheldon's inclination to use "eclectic" as a synonym for the words "original" and "modern."[18] "The style of the building is eclectic and modern," Sheldon wrote of the Pratt cottage (plate 29).[19] Although Scully is correct in pointing out that the term "eclectic" is a semantically incorrect substitution for "original," Sheldon chose a word that described many of these country houses well. Because most of these houses owe stylistic debts to diverse sources, categorizing them by style is often a frustrating and sometimes a futile undertaking.

Sheldon's open-mindedness, his tendency to accept almost all historical styles as equally useful for the American domestic architect, and his unwillingness to be negatively critical about any of the houses included in *Artistic Country-Seats* can be annoying to the modern reader. There was only one style that he castigated—the Queen Anne—and he did so repeatedly and without mercy. He called it "obsolete" and a "misnomer" to begin with. Furthermore, he was proud to announce that the houses he selected were free of its contamination. "One of the most inspiring facts revealed by the present collection of *Artistic Country-Seats* is the disappearance of the Queen Anne craze as a potent influence in American suburban architecture; and perhaps this fact was never so clearly demonstrated as in this portfolio of designs."[20] This is a perplexing statement, for Queen Anne elements can be seen in several of the photographs (plates 16 and 17, 34, 55, 59, for example). Scully explained Sheldon's aversion by pointing out that by 1886 the designation "Queen Anne" had become for conservative and eclectic critics a pejorative phrase meaning fashionable and transitory.[21]

Sheldon's Open-mindedness and Judgment

Did Sheldon really believe in the eclecticism he publicly endorsed? In the 1980s we may react suspiciously, wondering if his was not a false pluralism created to maintain the goodwill and feed the egos of all the families who lived in these variously designed houses. Possibly he was too close to the architectural scene to claim that one style was more suitable than all the rest. Possibly he reasoned that such a pronouncement might harm the current outburst of creativity. He may have believed that many types of country seats—small and large, cheap and expensive, rural and urban—legitimized stylistic variety. Whatever his reasons, he wrote positive judgments about houses that look quite different from one another.

For example, he liked simplicity. He praised Clarence Luce for designing the Josephs house (plate 11) for a moderate cost. "There is not a freak in the building anywhere. Everything is frank, candid, and rational. To provide a comfortable home by using the weather-toned old stones of the stern and rock-bound coast was the sole purpose."[22] Similarly, he liked the straightforwardness of the Pratt cottage (plate 29) at Manchester-by-the-Sea. "There is no sham ornamentation in Mr. Pratt's house—an air of honesty, simplicity, and suitableness prevails."[23] Of the Mallory house (plate 50), which contains signs of the Queen Anne style that upset him so much, he wrote "Mr. Mallory's cottage is introduced into this collection not because of its size, or costliness, or oddity, but because it is an example of a pure spirit in architecture—very simple, very broad in treatment, and erected at very little cost."[24] The Hemenway cottage (plate 49) by W. R. Emerson was so simple, strong and novel that few houses in the history of Western architecture could rival it. On the one hand, he could argue that "the most representative architects of the present era aim to find beauty less in added ornament than in such qualities as unity, fitness, and the interdependence of parts,"[25] but on the other hand, he delighted in descriptions of ornament, as in the case of the Appleton house (plate 15): "Very elaborate is the main cornice of the north elevation, the upper members being carved, with ornamental brackets and richly

carved frieze of decorative garlands, the treatment being very flat."[26] If he liked the Hemenway cottage because it was "novel," he also admired the "magnificent" private residence of Charles J. Osborn (plates 2 and 3), calling it "an immense modern feudal castle." He asked, what "fitness is there in erecting on the coast of Maine a Gothic or Italian villa," when complimenting the gambrel-roofed Smith house (plate 41), and then argued the advantages of "the old Scotch residence" when commenting on Henry C. Gibson's mansion (plate 20) outside of Philadelphia. Such contradictory positions are present throughout his commentaries. This can be supported most effectively by referring to the photographs themselves. Although these houses run the gamut of that period's artistic expression, Sheldon never said a harsh word about any of them. Scully did not respond warmly to Sheldon's catholicity of taste:

one should not take Sheldon's protestations in any direction too seriously. His perception is acute enough but he has no really solid body of principle, a general characteristic of thinking after the early 80's. . . . Furthermore, he was writing for the subscribers and felt it necessary to praise each house. . . . This is part of that peculiar spiritual bankruptcy which overwhelmed the later 80's and which eventually withered the very perceptions which enabled Sheldon at least to make the comments . . . [that American work had strong and striking features that were attracting the attention of European architects].[27]

But this was written 25 years ago. Today, while probably preferring the same houses that inspired Scully to write *The Shingle Style*, we would also be more likely to share Sheldon's appreciation of the diversity of artistic approaches in the 1880s and to thank him for acknowledging this diversity in photographs and plans. In addition, we would commend Sheldon for gathering disparate and often contradictory evidence of the architectural thought and sociological statements of the 1880s. Whether a house was graceful or gauche, it existed and was planned and executed for conscious and culturally important reasons.

Sheldon may be more vulnerable on another score—his judgment. His nineteenth-century sentences, heavy with commas and semicolons, conveying lofty ideals in decent phrases and relentlessly presenting an orderly and good world enlivened by progress, often obscured his material. Frequently, he made generalizations that sounded fine but were not applicable to the work of architecture he was discussing. Worse than that, he was often guilty of statements that were simply not true, statements that raise questions about his judgment or his memory. For example, he summarized the work of Arthur Little as follows:

He has a keen appreciation of the degraded condition of architecture, as exemplified by the greater number of the private residences of this country, and at the same time a perfect apprehension of the vitality and promise of the new era which has recently begun. Above all else, his buildings show us an eagerness to avoid anything that shall rank merely as an imitation of an art which was produced in ages inferior to our own, and at the same time to recognize the necessary continuity of the history of architecture. In nothing does he show a disposition to go off at a tangent.[28]

While this may be true of Little's Howe house (plate 88), it was not of the house he designed for his parents (plate 89). In "Grasshead" he playfully enlarged and isolated parts of the facade. Reacting to his tendency not to trim his trees before using them as porch columns, the *Builder* of London charged this was "an absurd affectation of rusticity which is at variance with architectural principles and good taste."[29] His architecture is appealing, in part, because he did go off on tangents. Sheldon's comments about the Kidder house (plate 92), an endearing collage of forms and textures, is another case in point. With more altruistic rhetoric than critical insight, he likened it to a "building skillfully adapted to its surroundings, designed in all its details and embellishments in accordance with true artistic feeling, and having an expression of harmony with the purposes for which it was constructed..."[30] Sheldon may have been caught between a publisher looking for profits and subscribers looking for compliments; nevertheless, he is not a reliable judge of architecture in *Artistic Country-Seats*.

Representative Commentaries

The commentaries accompanying these houses and casinos varied in length, amount of information and quality. The statements became progressively shorter; in Part One, Sheldon wrote eight descriptions of five or six pages in length while in the fifth part there was none that long. Roughly 34 of the 97 commentaries were well researched and contained extensive information about elevations, plans and settings. The best of these usually discussed the materials of the exterior, provided interior and exterior measurements, included accounts of the decoration of major rooms and personal reactions to the primary spaces. Occasionally, Sheldon addressed technical problems. He never included biographical information about the owners and only in one instance—the Stoughton house (plate 36) by Henry Richardson—did he discuss the career of the architect. A fine example of his best commentaries is the statement he wrote about the Isaac Bell, Jr. house (plate 7) at Newport. Five pages long in the original, it is quoted here in full:

This villa, built about four years ago, at Newport, by Messrs. McKim, Meade, and White, is of a modernized colonial style, the principal feature on the east front being the double gables, in one of which is an old treatment of triple windows. Each gable is thirty-two feet wide and twenty feet high from the eaves, and faced with cut shingles; and between them is a very elaborate leader-box of galvanized iron. There is also an elliptic window in the north gable. Three chimneys, the highest about twenty feet above the roof, are plainly treated, though one of them has an intricately-wrought iron brace, serving purposes both useful and ornamental. A glimpse of a tower on the south side also appears— but more of this further on. The windows in the gables all have small lights of glass, and above them are ornamental arches of carved wood.

The second story is of shingles, and the first story of brick. The piazza, extending across the whole width of the east front, is, on the north side, octagonal and two stories high, with an open balcony on the second floor and a shingled roof, and projecting eleven feet from the main piazza line, being twenty-two feet wide in all, with a total depth of twenty-five feet. At the south side, a small, square projection, eleven feet from the main piazza line, and sixteen feet wide, runs around the south side of the house, one story high, with a shingled gable, whose roof is supported on turned posts, having small projecting brackets at the upper portion. There is an entrance to the piazza on this east side, but the main entrance is on the south.

The extreme length of this south side is one hundred feet, the extreme length of the east side is eighty feet, and the extreme height of the building, including the tower, fifty-two feet. By far the principal feature of the south side is this tower—round, eighteen feet in diameter, of brick on the first floor, and shingled above. The entire first story of the house is of brick, the angles being finished with quoin-blocks of different-colored bricks. All the second story is shingled. A two-story window, with a carved wood panel between the upper and lower part, about on a line with the eaves of the main roof, constitutes a feature of the tower. All the courses of the roof have cut shingles, and there is a wrought-iron finial on the tower.

At the extreme east of the south side of the house is a small octagonal bay, with turned posts at each angle, and with small lights in all the sashes. Between the bay and the tower is an ornamental panel of diamond-shaped shingles. The piazza extends along the south side, from the tower to the east end, and one also sees the upper story of a north piazza. Instead of a railing, a brick wall receives the columns of the piazza, giving it a more substantial appearance. In the roof are two "winkers," which admit of a single pane of glass each, being more for ventilation than anything else, and accomplishing this object without introducing any hard lines, since they consist simply of a slight raising of the roof in two places. A noble chimney, twenty feet high and five feet wide, has a surface treated as a series of perpendicular ribs, projecting very slightly—just enough to get a simple shadow.

The main entrance is on the same side—an old-fashioned split door, heavily paneled. There is a landing-step for the convenience of those about to leave their carriages. Directly over the entrance the porch-roof projects in circular shape, being supported from the piazza-columns by ornamental brackets, in order to give protection from the rain, thus answering in part the purpose of a *porte-cochère*. To the west the kitchen wing is lower than the main building, and very simple in treatment, the first story of brick and the second of shingles. The roof of the house is shingled throughout.

Certain aspects of the interior of Mr. Bell's house deserve special mention. You enter a vestibule about nine feet by seven, containing an elaborate seat, and opening into the hall, thirty feet by twenty-four. At the right is a door into the reception-room, and beyond it one into the drawing-room. Directly opposite the entrance is the dining-room, and at the left of the entrance Mr. Bell's room, and between Mr. Bell's room and the dining-room, the staircase-hall. Considerable pains have been taken with the decoration of the main hall, while at the same time the effort has been to preserve simplicity. The finish is in oak, with a base eighteen inches high. Immediately around the fireplace is an extensive space of tiling, and a row of marble seats runs between the staircase and Mr. Bell's room. The mantel is of carved wood, and on either side of the fireplace is a small window of leaded glass, while in front of it stretches a hearth five feet wide, of red tile.

Opposite the staircase, eight feet wide, appears and open transom, supported on carved brackets. The cornice of the hall is very richly carved and molded, and in the front of the staircase a series of doors into the drawing-room can be rolled back, thus making the entrance-opening sixteen feet wide and eight feet high. To the right, a smaller door leads into the reception-room before mentioned. The dining-room doors are elaborately paneled, and a sheathed wainscoting eight and a half feet high gives height to the hall. A beautiful and much-carved screen, with panels of wood, separates the staircase from the fireplace, while over the fireplace the ceiling is lowered somewhat, being eight feet four inches instead of ten feet and a half, as in the main hall, in order to give a comfortably cozy look to the recess.

Standing at the dining-room door, and looking toward the vestibule, the entrance to the latter appears very wide—eight feet square, with an open lattice-work transom. To the right appears the door leading into Mr. Bell's room, and also the end of the fireplace recess, which is all tiled, with a large marble panel in the center. The dimensions of the dining-room are twenty feet by twenty-eight; it is paneled six feet high in mahogany, and above this, between the top molding of the wainscot and the cornice, are panels of rattan in the wall-spaces, and in each panel of rattan is a small square panel of perforated brass ornament—old curiosities collected by Mr. Bell. Very handsome is the mahogany cornice. The ceiling is treated like the side-walls—with a mahogany border three feet wide; separating this from the inner ceiling, which is divided into square panels, is a richly carved molding; while the inner ceiling itself is laid out in squares of rattan, two feet wide, by a very light molding. There are about sixty of these rattan squares, the central one being arranged for gas-fixtures. To the right of the room, as you enter, are three windows open to the floor and out into the octagonal piazza on the east side. On the opposite side the buffet is recessed in the wall, and divided into compartments for drawers, cupboards, shelves, and so on; the doors of the lower central part being elaborately carved, and all the hardware on them and on the drawers in antique brass of hammered and cut work. Directly above the buffet the space is finished in the form of a cove, with a shelf, supported on a small wooden bracket, running the whole width. Opposite the entrance-door, the fireplace, easily the chief feature of the room, has its lower part faced with marble, and a long low recess with a marble shelf above, while higher still the mantel proper is divided into three compartments which have glass doors, with a pattern in cathedral and square beveled plate glasses, the plan being a very flat octagonal, supported by two beautifully carved and turned posts at either side of the marble facing. Two windows at either side of the mantel open out into the yard at the north, and the upper part of their trim has a small balustrade, used for holding plates.

Mr. Bell's room shows a handsome mantel of painted pine, and a tile hearth two feet wide extending as far as the windows. A double window, opposite the entrance-door, has a seat, with drawers and lockers underneath. The entire left side of the apartment is filled with bookcases four and a half feet high, also of painted pine, the lower part being fitted up with drawers and the upper part with shelves. A simple sheathed wainscoting extends from the fireplace to the window, four and a half feet high. There is a wooden cornice, and about a foot below it a picture-strip.

In the drawing-room, the facing of the fire-opening is of tiles in a brass frame; above them projects the mantel-shelf proper, and higher still a beveled mirror in a handsome frame of carved wood. Below the mirror is a small shelf, supported on a number of carved brackets; and below the shelf an ornamental carved frieze of festoons and ribbons. To the left of the fireplace swings the heavily-paneled door of the dining-room; to the right a window opens out into the octagonal piazza. There is a base about two feet high, with its upper portion fluted; also a wooden cornice and picture-strip, between which runs a painted frieze of garlands and flowers, about a foot wide. Two windows, cut to the floor, open upon the east piazza opposite the entrance from the hall, and are five feet wide; while, opposite the fireplace, the trim of the sliding doors

into the reception-room consists of a projecting cornice of about six inches, supported on light carved brackets, there being also a small balustrade on the cornice itself. The wall-spaces are in silk; the wood-work throughout is pine, painted in white and gold. It may be added that painting is more common now than three years ago, when the rage was for "wood-fillers" and natural woods. Particularly in parlors and bedrooms, light effects are desired, but the rich dark tones of mahogany and oak are still considered suitable for dining-rooms and halls.

Mr. Bell's reception-room has a tiled opening, with a brass rim around its fireplace, and the mantel-shelf is handsomely carved, while the mantel extends up the height of the picture-strip, and is of wood. There is a base fifteen inches high, and the space between the picture-strip and cornice is a painted frieze of leaf-work. The cost of the house was about seventy-five thousand dollars.[31]

Unfortunately, the high quality and length of this discussion were not characteristic of the majority of the commentaries Sheldon wrote. About 38 of them offered a moderate amount of useful information, certainly much less than was written about the Bell house, and roughly 25 of them contained little useful material. When lacking the kind of detailed information he presented with the Bell house, Sheldon often filled in space with extended quotes from American or British architects or critics. Often these passages bore little direct relation to the house under consideration. An example of such a discussion, quoted in full, is his comment on the Laws house (plate 54) in Cincinnati.

We insert an illustration of Mr. Henry L. Law's [sic] house, on the Reading road, Cincinnati, Ohio, because of its extreme simplicity and solidity. The architect is Mr. James W. McLaughlin, the general style Romanesque, and the material blue limestone. The east elevation, which is shown in our illustration, has a porte-cochère on the north, a veranda, and a bold and massive effect. The roof is of slate, and the veranda of wood.

Little is to be said of the interior of Mr. Law's house; the hall is finished in oak, without wainscoting, the parlor in Canada maple, the dining-room and the library in cherry. Between the dining-room and the kitchen is a serving-room. There is an elevator at a convenient place, and the best kind of plumbing prevails. But much might be said of the simplicity and solidity of the design. "The worst faults of our architecture," observes an American architect, Mr. C. A. Cummings, "lie mostly in the direction of unrestrained or undisciplined ambition, which leads us, in the first place, to tell all we know, and sometimes more, at a single effort, as if we never expected another opportunity; and, secondly, to strive to produce, at all hazards, something startling and piquant, forgetting that the design, once executed, is to outlive all first impressions, and that what startles one to-day may disgust him to-morrow. Repose is contemned, and in its place we find the buildings, even of our educated architects, characterized too often by a fidgety and over-conscious display of knowledge, which might, under a stricter rule, have produced designs, if less striking at a first view, more admirable at every other. The young architect of to-day has only himself to blame if he has not the great examples of all styles and ages at his fingers' ends, as well as in his portfolios and scrap-books. His danger arises, not from want of technical knowledge, but from intemperance and disorder in the the use of it. The lightness and fickleness of our tastes, and their independence of fixed principles, lead us to follow the prevailing fashions of the day abroad—to design this year after the French Renaissance, next year after the English Gothic, next year, again, after the Queen Anne, so called. The performances, more or less striking, of European, especially of English artists, are promptly reported to us every week in the various journals, and we are as easily thrown off our balance by any audacious defiance of the plain rules of common sense or the requirements of common convenience, as by a real achievement of art. The French would say this is the natural and necessary result of the absence of an academic standard; and it is certain that there is something imposing in their steadfast adherence to a national style, and their thorough and trained performance in it. This is something impossible to us, and I am by no means sure that, in the long run, more is not lost than gained by it, even in France; but it would seem as if some mean might be discovered between a restraint so close as this and the wild license of our practice."[32]

Summary

Despite the flaws of *Artistic Country-Seats* which have been mentioned—Sheldon's loose definition of country seats, his high-sounding but vague phrases, his reluctance to offend, his inconsistent statements, his questionable evaluations, the unevenness of his descriptions and his habit of padding his text with dubiously relevant quotes—Sheldon's work is a remarkable achievement. There was no comparable survey in picture, plan and word of the American country house published in the mid-1880s. He provided subscribers and subsequent generations of architectural buffs with a wide-ranging survey at a significant moment in the evolution of the late nineteenth-century American life. His timing was impressive. He showed the vigor and imagination of the architectural profession, the skill of local contractors and the pride and means of those who owned these houses. His pictures connect us with a day and style of life that increasingly seem the work of fiction. His text provides information about interiors now altered or exteriors now removed. He and his publishers took pains to procure and to print excellent photographs and to provide readable plans. He undertook a heavy assignment, and his results were useful and beautiful.

NOTES

1. Vincent J. Scully, Jr., *The Shingle Style*, New Haven, 1955, 79–80, 170.
2. George William Sheldon, *Artistic Country-Seats: Types of Recent American Villas and Cottage Architecture with Instances of Country Club-Houses*, New York, 1886–87, vol. I, 41–42.
3. *Artistic Country-Seats*, vol. II, 4.
4. Frank H. Taylor, ed., *The City of Philadelphia*, Philadelphia, 1900, 220. Inexplicably, 40 of the photographs were printed in mirror image in *Artistic Country-Seats*. These mistakes have been corrected in this volume; the plans and photographs mesh. The photographs reversed in the original are plates 1–11, 13–19, 21, 24–33, 36, 39, 41, 46, 48–52, 54 and 57.
5. *Artistic Country-Seats*, vol. I, 44.
6. *Artistic Country-Seats*, vol. II, 186–187.
7. *Artistic Country-Seats*, vol. I, 153.
8. *Artistic Country-Seats*, vol. I, 155.
9. *Artistic Country-Seats*, vol. II, 64.
10. *Artistic Country-Seats*, vol. I, 71.
11. *Artistic Country-Seats*, vol. I, 72.
12. *Artistic Country-Seats*, vol. I, 68.
13. *Artistic Country-Seats*, vol. I, 43.
14. *Artistic Country-Seats*, vol. I, 43.
15. *Artistic Country-Seats*, vol. II, 68.
16. *Artistic Country-Seats*, vol. II, 93.
17. *Artistic Country-Seats*, vol. I, 167–168.
18. *The Shingle Style*, 100–101.
19. *Artistic Country-Seats*, vol. I, 128.
20. *Artistic Country-Seats*, vol. I, 220.
21. *The Shingle Style*, 103.
22. *Artistic Country-Seats*, vol. I, 46.
23. *Artistic Country-Seats*, vol. I, 129.
24. *Artistic Country-Seats*, vol. I, 217.
25. *Artistic Country-Seats*, vol. I, 141.
26. *Artistic Country-Seats*, vol. I, 62.
27. *The Shingle Style*, 110.
28. *Artistic Country-Seats*, vol. II, 142–143.
29. "Illustrations: American House Architecture," *Builder*, LII (Jan. 22, 1887), 148.
30. *Artistic Country-Seats*, vol. II, 157.
31. *Artistic Country-Seats*, vol. I, 23–27.
32. *Artistic Country-Seats*, vol. II, 13–14.

BIBLIOGRAPHY

Only sources mentioned or quoted in the captions have been included.

Books, Pamphlets and Dissertations

Cleveland Amory, *The Last Resorts*, New York, 1952.

——, *Who Killed Society?*, New York, 1960.

Antoinette F. Downing and Vincent J. Scully, Jr., *The Architectural Heritage of Newport, Rhode Island, 1640–1915*, New York, 1952.

W. Hawkins Ferry, *The Buildings of Detroit*, Detroit, 1968.

David Gebhard and Tom Martinson, *A Guide to the Architecture of Minnesota*, Minneapolis, 1977.

Louis H. Gibson, *Beautiful Houses: A Study in House-Building*, New York, 1895.

Mark Girouard, *Life in the English Country House*, New Haven, 1978.

——, *The Victorian Country House*, New Haven, 1979.

Samuel Huiet Graybill, Jr., "Bruce Price, American Architect, 1845–1903," 2 vols., Ph.D. dissertation, Yale University, New Haven, 1957.

Constance Harrison [Mrs. Burton], *Recollections Grave and Gay*, New York, 1916.

Cora L. Hartshorn, *A Little History of the Short Hills Section of Millburn Township, N.J. Developed by Stewart Hartshorn*, Millburn Public Library, 1964.

Henry-Russell Hitchcock, *The Architecture of H. H. Richardson and His Times*, Cambridge, 1961.

Wheaton Arnold Holden, "Robert Swain Peabody of Peabody and Stearns in Boston: The Early Years (1870–1886)," Ph.D. dissertation, Boston University, Boston, 1969.

S. F. Hotchkin, *Ancient and Modern Germantown, Mt. Airy, and Chestnut Hill*, Philadelphia, 1889.

Eric Johannesen, *Cleveland Architecture: 1876–1976*, Cleveland, 1979.

Sarah Bradford Landau, *Edward T. and William A. Potter, American Victorian Architects*, New York, 1979.

Lewis W. Leeds, *A Treatise on Ventilation*, New York, 1876.

Richard Longstreth, *Architecture in Philadelphia*, University of Pennsylvania Fine Arts Library, Philadelphia, 1968.

David Lowe, *Chicago Interiors: Views of a Splendid World*, Chicago, 1979.

Sidney Luska, *Mrs. Peixada*, New York, 1886.

A Monograph of the Works of McKim, Mead and White, 1879–1915, with an essay by Leland Roth, New York, 1973.

Oscar Newman, *Defensible Space*, New York, 1972.

David Nolan, "Villa Zorayda," in Florida Master Site File, Historic St. Augustine Preservation Board.

Dianne H. Pilgrim, "Decorative Art: The Domestic Environment," in *The American Renaissance: 1876–1917*, Brooklyn Museum, New York, 1979.

William B. Rhoads, *The Colonial Revival*, 2 vols., New York, 1977.

William Ganson Rose, *Cleveland: The Making of a City*, Cleveland, 1950.

E. K. Rossiter and F. A. Wright, *Modern House Painting, Containing Twenty Colored Lithographic Plates, Exhibiting the Use of Color in Exterior and Interior House Painting*, New York, 1882.

Leland M. Roth, *The Architecture of McKim, Mead and White, 1870–1920: A Building List*, New York, 1977.

——, "The Urban Architecture of McKim, Mead and White: 1870–1910," Ph.D. dissertation, Yale University, New Haven, 1973.

Ted Sande, *Theophilus P. Chandler*, seminar paper, University of Pennsylvania Fine Arts Library, 1971.

Vincent J. Scully, Jr., *The Shingle Style*, New Haven, 1955.

[George William Sheldon], *Artistic Houses*, 2 vols., New York, 1883–84.

Frank H. Taylor, ed., *The City of Philadelphia*, Philadelphia, 1900.

Edward Teitelman and Richard W. Longstreth, *Architecture in Philadelphia: A Guide*, Cambridge, 1974.

Douglass Shand Tucci, *Built in Boston: City and Suburb*, Boston, 1978.

Richard J. Webster, *Philadelphia Preserved*, Philadelphia, 1976.

Edith Wharton and Ogdon Codman, Jr., *The Decoration of Houses*, New York, 1978.

Elizabeth Biddle Yarnell, *Addison Hutton: Quaker Architect, 1834–1916*, with an essay by George B. Tatum, Philadelphia, 1974.

Cynthia Zaitzevsky, *The Architecture of William Ralph Emerson, 1833–1917*, Fogg Museum, Cambridge, 1969.

Articles

"American Villa Architecture," *Builder*, LI (Dec. 25, 1886), 907.

Wilhelm Bode, "Moderne Kunst in den Vereinigten Staaten von Amerika," *Kunstgewerbeblatt*, V (1894), 113–121 and 137–146.

Jean Boussard, "Mercantile Trust and Deposit Co., Baltimore, Maryland," *Le Moniteur des Architectes*, new ser., XX (1886), 48; "Architecture américaine: Types de porches," *Le Moniteur des Architectes*, new ser., XX (1886), 80; "Villa Mauresque en Amérique," *Le Moniteur des Architectes*, new ser., XX (1886), 128; and "Hôtel à Clifton," *Le Moniteur des Architectes*, new ser., XX (1886), 175.

"Discussion of Mr. Paterson's Paper," *Journal of the Royal Institute of British Architects*, ser. 3, V (Apr. 23, 1898), 328–331.

Georgian, "Georgian Homes of New England," *American Architect and Building News*, II (Oct. 20, 1877), 338–339.

Henry-Russell Hitchcock, "Frank Lloyd Wright and the 'Academic Tradition' of the Early Eighteen-Nineties," *Journal of the Warburg and Courtauld Institutes*, VII (1944), 46–63.

Wheaton A. Holden, "The Peabody Touch: Peabody and Stearns of Boston, 1870–1917," *Journal of the Society of Architectural Historians*, XXXII (May, 1973), 114–131.

"Illustrations: American House Architecture," *Builder*, LII (Jan. 22, 1887), 147–148.

Thomas W. Kelly and Joan Kelly, "A Street above Average: Summit Avenue, St. Paul," *Architecture Minnesota*, II (July–Aug., 1976), 33.

Julian Millard, "The Work of Wilson Eyre," *Architectural Record*, XIV (Oct., 1903), 282–325.

"New Germantown and Chestnut Hill," *Lippincott's Magazine*, XXXIII (Apr., 1884), 321–335.

"Newport Millionaires' Cottages," Liverpool *Evening Post* as reported in *American Architect and Building News*, LI (Mar. 28, 1896), 146.

Felix L. Oswald, "Healthy Homes," pt. 3, *Lippincott's Magazine*, XXXIII (Mar., 1884), 283–289.

R. S. Peabody, "The Georgian Houses of New England," *American Architect and Building News*, III (Feb. 16, 1878), 54–55.

Bruce Price, "The Suburban House," *Scribner's Magazine*, VIII (July, 1890), 3–19.

M. G. van Rensselaer, "American Country Dwellings," *Century Magazine*, XXXII (May, 1886), 3–20; (June, 1886), 206–220; and (July, 1886), 421–434.

M. G. van Rensselaer, "Recent Architecture in America," *Century Magazine*, XXVIII (July, 1884), 323–334.

R. Riordan, "Artists' Homes: Mr. Harry Fenn's, at Montclair, New Jersey," *Magazine of Art*, IX (1886), 45–48.

Paul Sédille, "American Architecture from a French Standpoint," *American Architect and Building News*, XX (Sept. 11, 1886), 122–124.

"Some Suburbs of New York," *Lippincott's Magazine*, XXXIV (July, 1884), 9–23.

"The S. P. Hinckley Houses," *Building*, IX (Sept. 29, 1888), 6 plates.

Walter Sturgis, "Arthur Little and the Colonial Revival," *Journal of the Society of Architectural Historians*, XXXII (May, 1973), 147–163.

"A Talk about Queen Anne," *American Architect and Building News*, II (Apr. 28, 1877), 133–134.

Lawrence Wodehouse, "William Appleton Potter, Principal Pasticheur of Henry Hobson Richardson," *Journal of the Society of Architectural Historians*, XXXII (May, 1973), 175–192.

W. S., "Amerikanische Landhäuser," *Deutsche Bauzeitung*, XXI (Sept. 10, 1887), 433–434.

LIST OF PLATES

Part One

1. Harry Fenn residence, Montclair, N.J.; H. Edwards Ficken, architect, 1884.
2 & 3. Charles J. Osborn residence, Mamaroneck, N.Y.; McKim, Mead & White, architects, 1885.
4 & 5. "Southside," Robert Goelet residence, Newport, R.I.; McKim, Mead & White, architects, 1883–84.
6. C. S. French residence, East Orange, N.J.; W. Halsey Wood, architect, n.d.
7. Isaac Bell, Jr. residence, Newport, R.I.; McKim, Mead & White, architects, 1883.
8. John W. Burgess residence, East Orange, N.J.; W. Halsey Wood, architect, 1881.
9. F. C. Geiger residence, East Orange, N.J.; W. Halsey Wood, architect, n.d.
10. Theodore F. Wood residence, Orange, N.J.; James Brown Lord, architect, n.d.
11. "Louisiana," Lyman C. Josephs residence, Middletown, R.I.; Clarence S. Luce, architect, 1883.
12. "Anglecot," Charles A. Potter residence, Philadelphia, Pa.; Wilson Eyre, Jr., architect, 1883.
13. "Sunnyridge," George W. Folsom residence, Lenox, Mass.; Charles C. Haight, architect, 1884.
14. Charles T. Cook residence, Elberon, N.J.; McKim, Mead & White, architects, 1885.
15. "Homestead," Julia Appleton residence, Lenox, Mass.; McKim, Mead & White, architects, 1884.
16 & 17. Newport Casino, Newport, R.I.; McKim, Mead & White, architects, 1880.
18. Herter residence, Monmouth Beach, N.J.; William B. Bigelow, architect, 1881.
19. "Seaverge," George F. Baker residence, Monmouth Beach, N.J.; Bruce Price, architect, ca. 1884.
20. "Maybrook," Henry C. Gibson residence, Wynnewood, Pa.; G. W. and W. D. Hewitt, architects, 1881.

Part Two

21. Samuel Colman residence, Newport, R.I.; McKim, Mead & White, architects, 1883.
22. "Farwood," Richard L. Ashhurst residence, Overbrook, Pa.; Wilson Eyre, Jr., architect, 1885.
23. Charles A. Newhall residence, Philadelphia, Pa.; Wilson Eyre, Jr., architect, ca. 1881.
24. J. H. Van Alen residence, Newport, R.I.; Clarence S. Luce, architect, n.d.
25. Joseph T. Low residence, Seabright, N.J.; Arthur B. Jennings, architect, 1885.
26. Short Hills Casino, Short Hills, N.J.; McKim, Mead & White, architects, 1880.
27. Henry P. Talmadge residence, Plainfield, N.J.; Douglas Smythe, architect, n.d.
28. Charles W. McCutchen residence, North Plainfield, N.J.; Charles H. Smith, architect, n.d.
29. William Pratt residence, Manchester-by-the-Sea, Mass.; Arthur Hooper Dodd, architect, 1883.
30. "Villa Zorayda," Franklin W. Smith residence, St. Augustine, Fla.; Franklin W. Smith, architect, 1883.
31. "Chatwold," G. B. Bowler residence, Bar Harbor, Me.; Rotch and Tilden, architects, 1883.
32. "Sunset Hall," Samuel P. Hinckley residence, Lawrence, N.Y.; Lamb and Rich, architects, 1883.
33. "Breakers," Cornelius Vanderbilt residence, Newport, R.I.; Peabody and Stearns, architects, 1877–78.
34. S. Bayard Dod residence, East Orange, N.J.; Arthur B. Jennings, architect, 1885.
35. "Ingeborg," William Simpson, Jr. residence, Wynnewood, Pa.; Theophilus P. Chandler, Jr., architect, 1884–85.
36. Mary F. Stoughton residence, Cambridge, Mass.; Henry H. Richardson, architect, 1883.
37. "Stonecliffe," Charles Taylor residence, Philadelphia, Pa.; Theophilus P. Chandler, Jr., architect, 1880–81.
38. "Restrevor," Samuel B. Brown residence, Haverford, Pa.; Theophilus P. Chandler, Jr., architect, 1881–84.
39. "Kragsyde," George Nixon Black residence, Manchester-by-the-Sea, Mass.; Peabody and Stearns, architects, 1884.
40. Edwin N. Benson residence, Philadelphia, Pa.; Theophilus P. Chandler, Jr., architect, 1884.

Part Three

41. James Hopkins Smith residence, Falmouth Foreside, Me.; John Calvin Stevens, architect, 1885.
42. "Ballytore," Isaac H. Clothier residence, Wynnewood, Pa.; Addison Hutton, architect, 1885.
43. P. E. Van Riper residence, Montclair, N.J.; Francis H. Kimball, architect, 1884–86.
44. Addison G. Foster residence, St. Paul, Minn.; Clarence H. Johnston, architect, 1883.
45. Potter Palmer residence, Chicago, Ill.; Cobb and Frost, architects, 1885.
46. Chauncey W. Griggs residence, St. Paul, Minn.; Clarence H. Johnston, architect, 1883.
47. Sylvester T. Everett residence, Cleveland, O.; Charles F. Schweinfurth, architect, 1883.
48. Frederick Driscoll residence, St. Paul, Minn.; William H. Willcox, architect, 1884.
49. Mary Hemenway residence, Manchester-by-the-Sea, Mass.; William R. Emerson, architect, 1884.
50. Henry R. Mallory residence, Bryam, Conn.; Lamb and Rich, architects, ca. 1885.
51. "Mossley Hall," William B. Howard residence, Mount Desert, Me.; William R. Emerson, architect, 1883.
52. Narragansett Pier Casino, Narragansett Pier, R.I.; McKim, Mead & White, architects, 1886.
53. Henry A. C. Taylor residence, Newport, R.I.; McKim, Mead & White, architects, 1886.
54. Harry L. Laws residence, Cincinnati, O.; James W. McLaughlin, architect, ca. 1886.

AMERICAN
COUNTRY HOUSES
OF THE GILDED AGE
(Sheldon's "Artistic Country-Seats")

1. Harry Fenn residence, Montclair, N.J.; H. Edwards Ficken, architect, 1884. In 1885 the *Magazine of Art* (London) published an article about this house, recently completed for the watercolorist and illustrator Harry Fenn. There were two reasons for this article. For one thing, Fenn was well known in England. Born in Richmond, Surrey, in 1838, he settled in the United States in 1857 but retained close ties with his native country, where his sketches were seen frequently in the popular magazines of the day and also in several books, among them *Picturesque America* and *Picturesque Europe*. Secondly, the journal used the opportunity to acknowledge the rising quality of American architecture. "Now, although the younger architects of America, as might be expected of men who have broken with tradition, have quite generally fallen into an unchastened, mongrel style, full of affectations and overladen with bad ornament, still this much may be said for them, that they have almost as generally sought to secure comfort and convenience as well as a picturesque outline, and a warm and harmonious scheme of colour as well as an abundance of rather cheap decoration." Fenn's house, standing today at 208 North Mountain Avenue, probably appealed to British readers because of its half-timbered work and its colors — dark clapboards and stained cypress shingles. The British usually reacted negatively to the "chilly" white so popular for framed houses. According to the contract, the cost of the residence, exclusive of interior decoration, was only $8,250. This view shows the approach to the house with the servants' stairway to the left and the principal entrance to the right. Rarely were these two entrances placed so close to one another or the servants' stairway so visible from the public side of a house. The far side contained a piazza and several balconies from which one could see Coney Island as well as the highlands of the Hudson River. Under the gambrel roof of the attic floor was Fenn's studio. The sleeping floor consisted of six bedrooms, a bathroom, sewing room and linen closet. The dining room, hall and parlor were spacious rooms with wide openings between them, enabling visitors to appreciate the delicate or-

chestration of room colors—light salmon, cream and warm gray, respectively. Fenn decorated these rooms with objects collected during his frequent travels—white Delft and Moorish platters, Nankin blue-and-white porcelain, drawings by Burne-Jones, gilt leather from Japan, a chest dated 1639 found in a barn in England. Ficken's career is not well documented. A native of London who was educated at Greenock Academy in Scotland, he practiced in New York City for about 50 years and died there in January, 1927. In 1883 he designed a new store for Van Tine & Co., Japanese importers, which may account for the Japanese-influenced woodwork of the Fenn house.

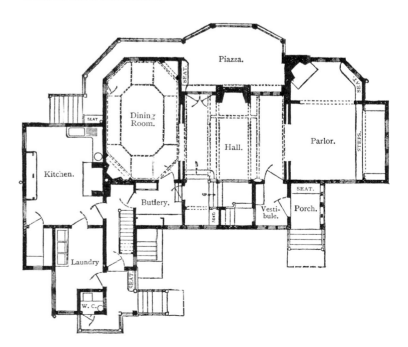

2 and 3. Charles J. Osborn residence, Mamaroneck, N.Y.; McKim, Mead & White, architects, 1885. Although there is no discernible system behind Sheldon's arrangement of the 97 plates of houses and casinos in *Artistic Country-Seats*, he may have had two reasons for choosing the Osborn residence as the first to be illustrated. (See the Preface for a discussion of the original order of the Plates.) He had a weakness for huge country houses and for this one in particular; "no more magnificent private residence exists in this country than that of the late Mr. Charles J. Osborn, at Mamaroneck, on Long Island Sound." Furthermore, it was designed by the firm of McKim, Mead & White, one of the foremost architectural offices of the 1880s, the most influential in designing houses in the period from which Sheldon made his selections, and the firm illustrated more frequently (16 times) in his anthology than any other. His open-minded outlook embraced shingled cottages as well as ostentatious mansions, but he was frequently impressed, as in this instance, by houses that were large, expensive, well furnished and functionally modern but artistically respectful of history. The length of the house facing the Sound was 153′ and its widest depth was 144′. The semirectangular main portion was 125′ × 76′, permitting principal rooms of spacious dimensions: hall (25′ × 31′), parlor (20′ × 25′), reception room (18′ × 15′), dining room (21′ × 30′), staircase hall (18′ × 12′) and billiard room (20′ × 21′). Located in the tower above the parlor, the master bedroom was 22′ in diameter with an attached dressing room (14′ × 9′). Leland Roth reported the cost of the house as $181,310, and Sheldon estimated the final bill for house, grounds, greenhouses, stables,

farmer's house and gate lodge to be approximately $400,000. As was true of the majority of the most expensive houses in this series, the percentage of the final costs spent on the woodwork and interior detail was significant. According to Sheldon, the main hall "has two stories, and is of unusual size, being . . . twenty-five feet high. Very important is the mantel-piece, two stories high, the fireplace so large that you could almost drive a horse in, and the single flue enormous. The dimensions of the fire-opening are—width, six feet; height, six feet; depth, two feet four. A wind-gauge, worked in as a part of the design of the mantel-piece, connects with the weather-vane high up on the hall-chimney outside. The paneled wainscoting has elaborate carved moldings of English oak, finished in natural color. To the left of the fireplace a wide seat, with casement-windows opening out on the Sound, and near it an ornamental niche, constitutes a striking feature." White, responsible for the interior, generally followed contemporary practice in selecting the wood to be used in each of the main rooms. His choice of oak for the hall was not surprising. To show the social importance of both parlor and dining room, he chose white mahogany and Santo Domingo mahogany, respectively. While American parlors and dining rooms were often expensively finished, these woods were not used commonly. Painted pine was a very modest wood for White to use in the reception room. Also, its color scheme of white and gold was more delicate than one would have expected in such a ponderous dwelling. The house was also planned to be convenient and comfortable. For example, there were two hot-air furnaces and in the main basement a veg-

etable storage room, laundry, bathroom and the coal and wine
cellars. Under the winter quarters at the west end, separated from
the main body of the house by the porte-cochere, was a separate
basement with a kitchen. Osborn probably used the winter quarters during the two or three days he enjoyed the house between
its completion and his death in November 1885. Finally, the design owed much to history. The exterior was unusually heavy for
a country house by McKim, Mead & White and its great stone
towers and conical roofs intentionally recalled Norman architecture of the eleventh and twelfth centuries. Vincent Scully suggested that, living there, "the client is meant to feel himself a
baron." The partnership of Charles Follen McKim (1847–1909),
William Rutherford Mead (1846–1928) and Stanford White
(1853–1906), formed in 1879, was responsible for 785 separate
commissions between that date and 1909, when McKim died.
Their country houses in the period represented in *Artistic Country-Seats*, 1878–87, illustrate their consistent leadership in the
transformation of American domestic work. So important was their
role that one is tempted to see the evolution of their plans and
elevations as a summary of what occurred nationally. After he
entered Wall Street in 1865, Osborn became the private broker
of Jay Gould and established his own firm of C. J. Osborn & Co.,
which survived the panic of 1873. A noted yachtsman, owner of
the "Dreadnaught" and the steam yacht "Corsair," he retired in
1883 but died before he reached 50. A fire in 1971 partially destroyed the building, now owned by the Mamaroneck Beach, Ca-
bana and Yacht Club.

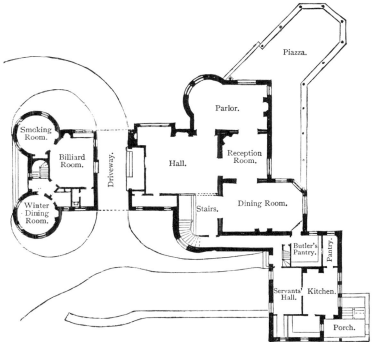

4 and 5. "Southside," Robert Goelet residence, Newport, R.I.; McKim, Mead & White, architects, 1883–84. Still standing at the corner of Narragansett and Ochre Point Avenues, "Southside" was one of ten Newport buildings which Sheldon selected for *Artistic Country-Seats*, six of which were designed by McKim, Mead & White. It is a remarkable house, for its expression depends upon characteristics that are potentially contradictory—scale, elegance, wealth and self-confidence on the one hand and energy, change, vernacular complexity and informality on the other. Perhaps the public facade (above) suffers because the central symmetrical section is too high-toned and becomes detached from its supporting cast, and perhaps the quickness and lightness of the superb piazza of the oceanside (opposite) are not sustained in the middle of the upper stories, but the risks White, the principal architect, has taken have, nevertheless, produced rich results. One of the most obvious was to create one house with two distinct faces, a more formal side facing the street and a less formal side facing the ocean. Of the two, the latter is more stimulating because the appendages, which White pulled from the long quiet body of the house, look cohesive rather than adhesive, despite appearing to be lively or robust. He contrasted their physicality against the darkness, emptiness and mystery of the voids, and thus exploited the known and the unknown as well as advancing and receding sections to enrich

his design. Brick was used for the first story and shingles, laid in wavy layers on the dormers and the gables of the piazza and in diamond and circle designs elsewhere, covered the walls and the roof. The rippling of these surfaces complement the activity of the forms they define. However, in 1886 Mariana van Rensselaer, a perceptive architectural critic, questioned the appropriateness of shingles for a house which was so imposing. "But there are certainly cases when, however it may be blent with other factors, the shingle seems a mistake. . . . For example, I think it is out of keeping both with the design and with the interior in Mr. Goelet's house on the Newport Cliff. . . . Such an interior, so large, so dignified, so sumptuous and refined in decoration, is not fittingly to be sheathed in shingles. And while the design, already too heavy, too massive in effect for the place it holds, would have looked still heavier had it been executed in sterner materials, yet nevertheless as a design judged in the abstract (judged intrinsically, without reference to site and purpose and surroundings) it would, I think, have greatly been the gainer." Designs may be judged in the abstract, but they should not be built in the abstract. The choice of shingles obviously was influenced by the spectacular natural site, by the function of the house as a summer "cottage," and because the Goelets, confident about themselves and their social status, did not require a more substantial and expensive material.

Through the raised platform covered with grass, White integrated the house and site on both sides, but his integration was exceptionally fine on the ocean side where the rise of the lawn anticipates the steps. Recent pictures of the house, denuded of plants and ivy, make clear how important they were in reinforcing this integration. The hall unquestionably controlled the interior spatially and artistically. Sheldon's description was very informative: "Entering the building, the spectator is at once attracted and delighted by the magnitude and the beauty of the main hall, which is forty-four feet long, thirty feet wide, and twenty-four feet high—a size very seldom seen in a villa on this side of the water—and the taste and luxury with which it has been finished and furnished are not less noteworthy. The immense chimney-piece extends two stories high, and the fireplace is large enough for a man to walk into. A gallery, supported on a series of columns and open arches, extends around the second story, and the ceiling shows the open timber-work. One of the arches forms an entrance to the main staircase; and on the other side of the fireplace is a large square opening into the parlor. Up to the line of the second story the entrance-hall is paneled solid with oak, and the balustrade of the gallery is of turned spindles of the same wood, those of the projecting balcony in the center, directly opposite the chimney-piece, being in a line slightly curving outward." Robert Goelet (1841–1899)

was a New York realtor who had inherited part of his father's fortune, also made in New York real estate. Leland Roth reported that the house cost \$83,488; Sheldon claimed \$200,000, which probably included property, landscaping and interior decoration.

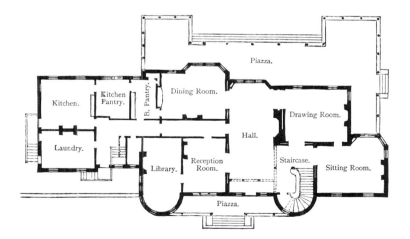

6. C. S. French residence, East Orange, N.J.; W. Halsey Wood, architect, n.d. This was not a summer or country house, but a suburban residence in one of the many attractive north Jersey towns which grew rapidly in the late nineteenth century. If designers of country dwellings could take advantage of unpopulated acres and delightful, if not spectacular, scenery, the city architect usually had to cope with restricted lots on a gridiron street plan. Nevertheless, architectural expression was still obligatory. In this design Wood made clear that the house must protect those who lived within. For a house to make such a statement in a community where neighbors were expected to trust neighbors was socially risky. Therefore, the architect had to include features that would counteract this antisocial impression. The curving steps made an overture to pedestrians. Though the entrance porch was dark, its arch was generously wide. The severity of the right side of the house was complemented by the activity of the left, where balconies and oriel windows provided plenty of opportunity for those within to acknowledge the neighborhood. The woodwork, in places suggesting interior finish mistakenly placed outside, and the arbitrary shapes of the shingle-covered forms suggest that Wood may have tried to counteract the raw, powerful statement of the brick walls. Nevertheless, this was a most unusual and striking house, a distinctive manifestation of the design tendencies of the early 1880s. Inside, the vestibule led to a hall (14′ × 15′), the rear part of which was elevated one foot. The fireplace, stairway and dining room were on this higher level. Sixteen feet in diameter, the dining room contained a curving mantel and window seat and was furnished with a large round table. On the second floor were three bedrooms, a bathroom, sewing room and several closets, while the attic floor was divided into one large bedroom and a servant's room. A well-equipped laundry was located in the base-

ment. Records indicate that construction and decoration costs amounted to $5,640, broken down into bills of $1,935 for the mason, $2,930 for the carpenter, $150 for heating, $424 for plumbing and $200 for interior decoration. Erected at Arlington and Park Avenues for French, a dealer in coal and wood, the house has been razed. The architect (1855–1897) was born in Newark where he studied and opened his first office at the age of 24 after an apprenticeship with Thomas A. Roberts. An accomplished draftsman, Wood was best known for his exuberant ecclesiastic designs.

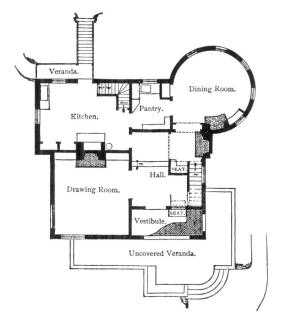

7. Isaac Bell, Jr. residence, Newport, R.I.; McKim, Mead & White, architects, 1883. This house, which appears to be comfortable and pleasant, is enlivened quietly by gracious curves and is well integrated with its natural surroundings. We may tend to underestimate it because it seems so undemonstrative, so effortless, so inevitable. Similarly, the plan expands unhurriedly and without complication from a generous hall toward vantage points where the landscape can be enjoyed. Inside and out, this classic statement of the shingle style brilliantly expresses the possible ideal—the good summer life for society's blessed in an era of unlimited national and personal promise. The confidence of its owners and designers in the world they understood is present in the encircling piazza and the second-story porch, those semipublic regions of a house which encourage seeing and being seen. Without compromising the core of the house, these verandas are gestures of good will. Further proof of this confidence is evident in the plan's centrifugal movement and the unpretentious and physically vulnerable shingles that contain its expanding volumes. This was a bold artistic venture. The designers rejected the safe road—order, dignity, proven solutions—in favor of spatial excitement, contrasts (texture and void), variations (multiple shingle patterns), asymmetry of perimeter and skyline, and mixed materials (brick below and shingles above). Something ventured, something gained—namely a creation that continues to become rather than one designed to be: paradoxically, a transient architecture. The eye is attracted by two kinds of movement, the rippling of the surface and the slower pace set by the large, plastic forms. Within, it is the latter that characterizes the flow of space from the pivotal hall toward the light of adjacent rooms. Though the sensation of change is present, the dominant impression of the interior is that of warmth, comfort and low-key luxury. These are set forth strongly at the core of the house, the great hearth, stretching from study to stairs, with a wide chimney and fine paneling on three sides and a wood ceiling two feet lower than that of the hall proper. The stairway, seen through an opening at the end of the hearth,

was, like the other spaces of this floor, ample and calm. To the designers' credit, they protected the rectangular integrity and openness of the hall (30′ × 24′) by renouncing the easy effect of an intruding stairway. Isaac Bell, Jr. (1846–1889) paid approximately $41,000 for this house (Sheldon claimed $75,000) which measured 100′ × 80′ and, to the top of the tower, was 52′ high. Supported by his father's fortune, he was personally successful in the cotton trade in New Orleans and New York. He married and retired the same year, 1877, when he was 31 years old. President Cleveland appointed him ambassador to the Netherlands in 1885. The house still stands on Bellevue Avenue. (For Sheldon's description of the house, see the text.)

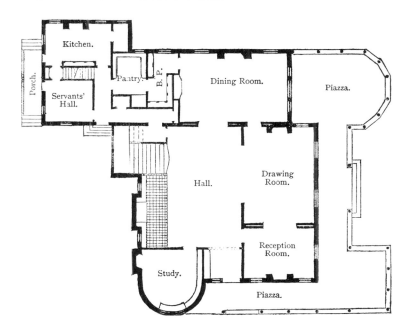

8. John W. Burgess residence, East Orange, N.J.; W. Halsey Wood, architect, 1881. The decade of the 1880s was one of the most creative in the history of American domestic architecture not only in design but also in technology. The science of house construction improved rapidly after the Civil War, partly because of increased attention to engineering programs in major universities and technical schools. The market was crowded with new patents and products claiming to save labor, cut costs and perform more efficiently and dependably. Sold to the public before adequate testing, the inventions and discoveries often were more impressive in their advertisements than in their performance. The Burgess house contained several well-advertised schemes for overcoming traditional problems. To stop the flaking of brickwork, caused by winter frost and summer dampness, the owner spent $4,000 for a paraffin seal burned one quarter of an inch into the brick. In addition, this sealant was supposed to preserve the warm color of the brick more effectively and to prevent staining. Canvas, instead of the usual tin, covered the lengthy floor of the balcony. It was supposed to keep the sun from heating the surface excessively and to protect the second-floor windows from glare. To stop water from dripping onto the veranda below, the canvas was covered with four coats of paint. Much attention in this period was also given to the plumbing and sewer systems. Because leaks in newly installed plumbing were common, architects tried to make the pipes as accessible as possible. Exposed hardware under a sink was considered a practical virtue and not an artistic gaffe. One wonders why the pipes of this house, placed "entirely on the outside of the building, where all the pipes are in plain sight," did not freeze in the East Orange winters. A family's fear of fire or tornado was but a mild concern compared to the terror generated by the thought of "deadly sewer gas." One could see and address a leaking pipe but not the invisible threat of escaping gas. Wood installed a variant of a cesspool system, numerous pipes three or four feet below the surface that carried wastes to the end of the sloping backyard. Constructed for approximately $33,000, this res-

idence (96' × 50'), located at 34 Munn Avenue according to the Orange Directory of 1882, has been demolished. Its veranda was one of the longest of the houses in this book and its balcony, probably the longest, enabled the family to promenade without leaving home. The basement, second and third floors were finished in ash and the first floor in sycamore, which possessed a rich grain and, when rubbed, produced a variety of tints. None of the interior woodwork was painted. The entire mantel of the drawing room was composed of mirrors which reflected the long space that passed through the three front rooms. The special attraction of the landing was a stained-glass window by Charles Booth of London.

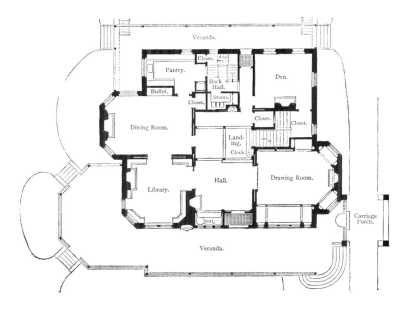

9. F. C. Geiger residence, East Orange, N.J.; W. Halsey Wood, architect, n.d. This was one of three houses by Wood in *Artistic Country-Seats* (see plates 6 and 8) which reveal his organizational and artistic tendencies. The hall, usually centrally located, was reached through a vestibule somewhat darkened by its protective porch. Regular-shaped rooms, defined by thick walls and connected to other rooms by sliding doors, surrounded this hall. He often attempted to round off his boxlike plans by including curving forms (a room or concentric steps) or octagonal forms (window or porch) at the corners. Outside, he demonstrated a predilection for semi-elliptical arches over entranceways, windows and porch bays, railings with closely set balusters and high continuous roof ridges. He utilized randomly laid brick or stone to create an aged appearance, and he depended upon unifying horizontals to incorporate isolated details. Of the three houses, the design for the now-demolished Geiger house, which stood on Central Avenue between Munn Avenue and Harrison Street, was probably the most representative of the larger domestic scene. The relationship between the first floor—of mountain traprock and rare shingling under the veranda—and the upper floors, sheathed in shingles, was stronger than in the Burgess house and its windows and projections were integrated more successfully than in the French house. Despite common features, the three were sufficiently dissimilar to suggest the hand of three different architects. If these houses demonstrated Wood's versatility and possibly his experimental attitude toward self-discovery, they also revealed his ability to design distinctively in several different styles. The colors chosen for the original house sound appealing: windows and doors of the main floor were outlined in warm red brick, the entrance steps were rubbed blue stone, the second-floor shingles were stained with creosote for protection and for an appearance of age, and the chimneys were constructed of red and buff brick. Within, the hall (21′ × 12′) contained panels of ash, which was also used for the staircase and the mantels while the remaining woodwork of the interior was of pine, filled and stained, in part accounting for the modest cost of $6,000. Wood's career was shortened by consumption a few years after his apparent victory in the St. John the Divine Cathedral competition was successfully challenged by a Columbia professor who argued its great lantern was too heavy for the structure to carry. His wife touchingly recalled his moment of glory in 1891. "The rooms were crowded; Halsey Wood's name was on everyone's lips. I stood for some time waiting for him, in the midst of an excited throng, while the cry, 'Where are Halsey Wood's designs?' rang out continuously from those about me." Though unexecuted, the drawings for "Jerusalem the Golden" are spectacular examples of late nineteenth-century American draftsmanship.

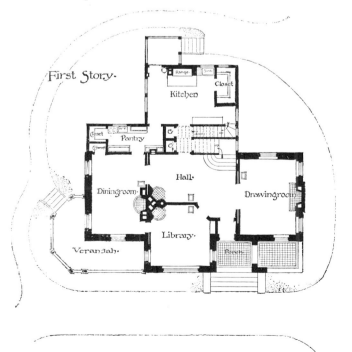

10. Theodore F. Wood residence, Orange, N.J.; James Brown Lord, architect, n.d. This house stood on Highland Avenue near the railroad station in Orange. According to regional directories, Wood moved into the house sometime after 1882, probably in 1885. Lord's facade was based primarily on three compositional means. His main vehicle was fenestration. The variety of windows within one facade is impressive—round and elliptical, vertical and horizontal, windows in series and windows in isolation, and windows at various levels within one floor. He utilized the gable, that architectural form which was probably more important than any other in creating the distinctive appearance of American suburban houses in the early 1880s. Here the projection of the gable is crucial because the second- and first-floor walls are almost planar. Only the walls of the laundry, recessed to provide more light for the dining room, broke the flatness of these two floors. The sloping roof of the gable at the right side of the photograph continued downward, terminating in the partially obscured servants' porch. Although the raking cornice of the other side was not carried into the second story, we nevertheless tend to see a gigantic triangle outlining this section of the house. Although such dramatic compositional devices were popular with designers in the United States, some Europeans questioned them. The eminent French architect Paul Sédille wrote from Paris in 1886, "Sometimes your country houses appear to be no more than lumbering peasants' houses buried under enormous roofs. The low ground floors seem plunged into the shade of porticoes, verandas and projections of every kind which envelop the construction." Finally, Lord set two stories of wood on a base of stone. There were many reasons for this common arrangement: artistic possibilities increased in color, texture and materials, the house appeared more stable than one constructed entirely of wood, greater protection was provided at the public level and it was much cheaper than a house of brick or stone. Compare, for example, the time and effort required to set the stones of the arch of the dining-room wall with the time and effort required to cut the arch in wood of the third floor. The house measured 61' long without the piazzas and 32' deep; the cost of its construction was approximately $12,000. Like many of the architects included in this series, Lord (1859–1902) came from a well-established Eastern family, and family connections undoubtedly influenced the commissions he received. He designed houses for Pierre Lorillard's Tuxedo Park and restaurants for the Delmonico family. His most important commission was the Appellate Division Courthouse, Madison Square in New York City, designed in 1896.

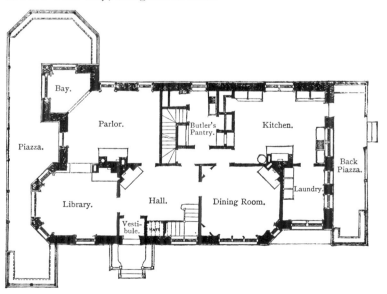

11. "Louisiana," Lyman C. Josephs residence, Middletown, R.I.; Clarence S. Luce, architect, 1883. Sheldon noted in this design a "certain Flemish feeling," and contemporary architectural historians would probably cite Dutch Colonial design as a source of inspiration. American designers, unquestionably, drew heavily upon a European past that was not directly theirs in their efforts to shape a domestic architecture suitable for the 1880s. Of course, this had been done since the seventeenth century. In one of his wiser observations, Sheldon wrote that the difference he detected was that contemporary designers were now doing so with much more self-confidence and practicality than ever before. They subordinated adopted forms sensibly to "practical and social conditions, and thus have created certain peculiarities of form and style." The result, he concluded, was "that certain forms peculiar to ourselves, and capable of a higher degree of artistic development, have been produced." Despite these debts to the past, the Josephs house was peculiarly American. The use of the stones, taken from an old wall on the premises, revealed a practical and flexible approach to architecture. Their natural features, enriched "by the hand of Time," produced a foundation that could not be accused of being precious or too intellectual. Americans, especially those on vacation, were proud to stay close to the bountiful land with which they were blessed and were confident enough to weaken sturdy walls with windows and porches that enabled them to see the land's beauties. The length of the house, 150', was probably encouraged by the false assumption that American space was limitless. The simple clarity of the precisionist strain in American art is visible in the roof and the spare forms that project from it. While it is true that the stones commemorate a given place, the unbroken eave of the roof glorifies movement within the structure and even beyond it. This house illustrates extremely well a conflict that became clearer as the decade progressed. It was the conflict between the centrifugal interior, composed of spaces that left the impression of moving from the center outward, and the growing preference for the symmetrical elevation. The interiors spoke for process and irregularity; the elevations for being and order. Here the remarkable abstract and geometric perimeter frustrates the aspirations of the plan. Sheldon reassured readers that the smells of the stables, rarely located under the same roof with humans in American practice, did not reach the family, and then proceeded, matter-of-factly, to report that the servants slept over the carriage house and stalls. Built for only $10,200 and still standing on Wolcott Avenue, this was the summer house of Lyman Josephs of Baltimore, regarded at his death in 1942, at the age of 88, as the longest continuous summer resident of the Newport area.

12. "Anglecot," Charles A. Potter residence, Philadelphia, Pa.; Wilson Eyre, Jr., architect, 1883. Though Eyre was born in Florence, Italy in 1858, his parents were Philadelphians of means. After a year of studying architecture at M.I.T., he worked under Joseph P. Sims from 1878 until 1881, when Sims died, and Eyre began to practice independently. One of several outstanding Philadelphia architects of the late nineteenth and early twentieth centuries (others were Frank Day, Walter Cope, John Stewardson and Frank Furness), Eyre is best known today for the distinctive houses he built in the suburbs of the city. He died in 1944. Julian Millard, reviewing his work for *Architectural Record* in October, 1903, wrote that his "strong individuality, amounting almost to eccentricity, has resulted in many peculiarities, not all of which are agreeable." "Anglecot," spiced with eccentricities, is quite agreeable. Although it is categorized as a shingle-style house, much of its surface is not covered with shingles. The first story is brick and the projecting sections are hung with tiles that complement the texture of the wood. While Eyre arranged "normal" windows brilliantly to flood certain rooms with light, he also enjoyed the carefully placed, oddly shaped window that was as much an artistic as an illuminating factor. Placing gable on top of gable, he created the impression of advancing planes. The lighter stucco decoration by sculptor John J. Boyle and the plaster sundial below, seen against a darker background, reinforced this impression. Despite these projections, Eyre sustained the dominant planarity of the facade. The fence and gate inhibited trespassers but not the curious, who were free to contemplate the white, raised platform—a special place for special people. At the rear of the platform Eyre created a humorous dialogue between the tight doorway, thrust forward, and the choir bench pulled back into the broad cavity. This niche is the vestige of the front porch, that social as well as architectural institution which disappeared from domestic work in the twentieth century because attitudes toward the social environment changed. Anticipating the porch's demise and the rise of the backyard as the preferred location for family relaxation, Eyre placed the veranda on the private side of the house. Within, the dining area was cleanly separated from the living area of hall and parlor by the stairway hall. Richard Longstreth has pointed out that the "built-in cabinetry is exceptional," reminding us that American architects of the day were quite willing to incorporate furniture and conveniences such as sideboards, china closets, chimney seats and closets. The house, known today as Anglecot Nursing Home, is located at the corner of Evergreen Street and Prospect Avenue in Chestnut Hill. It was built for $12,000 by Thomas Potter, Jr. of Thomas Potter & Sons, oilcloth and linoleum manufacturers, for his son Charles.

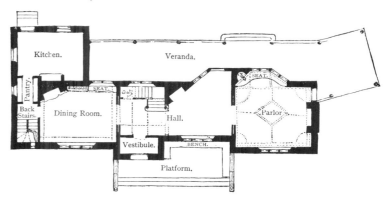

13. "Sunnyridge," George W. Folsom residence, Lenox, Mass.; Charles C. Haight, architect, 1884. The Folsom house, magnificently located overlooking the Stockbridge Bowl at what is today 49 Cliffwood Street, burned in 1925 but was rebuilt the following year. The original structure had a clapboard first level, shingles above and on the roof, and timber work in the gables. Sheldon called it "Early English" and explained that it had been designed after a house that formerly stood on the site. The plan contained several unusual features. The main hall was perpendicular to the principal entrance, and its stairway was located in the corner and not toward the center of the family area. For a summer house the doorways into the library and dining room were exceptionally narrow. The boudoir behind the chimney of the drawing room was atypical, as was the interrupted space of the library. Moderately furnished, the hall was done in quartered oak, the drawing room in white pine polished but not painted, and the library in black walnut. During the 1880s, Lenox, "the Newport of the Berkshires," was attracting cottagers who were wealthier and less intellectually inclined than its earlier summer residents. Mrs. Burton Harrison summarized this transformation in *Recollections Grave and Gay.* "The rural hillsides and pastures, bought up at fabulous prices, were made the sites of modern villas, most of them handsome and in good taste. The villas were succeeded by little palaces, some repeating the facades and gardens of royal dwellings abroad. Instead of the trim maidservants appearing in caps and aprons to open doors, one was confronted by lackeys in livery lounging in the halls. Caviar and *mousse aux truffes* supplanted muffins and waffles." By 1886 large summer houses, spaciously protected by properties of ten to 500 acres, dotted the beautiful, sloping country. Buying views became more important than buying land, and, according to a reporter of 1887, the "comparison of views is the chief occupation of the resident summer population." This resort, perhaps more than any other, was the antithesis of the city: safe, rural, quiet, unpopulated and exclusive. In a period when the aristocracy of wealth flaunted its superiority and lists of acceptable and unacceptable families were common, Lenox was

an ideal haven. Even the *New York Times* (August 21, 1887) approvingly pointed out that "the vermin of civilization do not infest it. The organ grinder and his 'leetle monk' is not here." Charles Coolidge Haight (1841–1917) was a "gentleman of the old school," courtly in manner, artistically conservative and older than most of the architects included in this series. For his alma mater, Columbia, he designed the School of Mines building (1874) and Hamilton Hall (1880) on the University's Midtown Campus. Between 1885 and 1900 he built many buildings in New York City, particularly hospitals and churches.

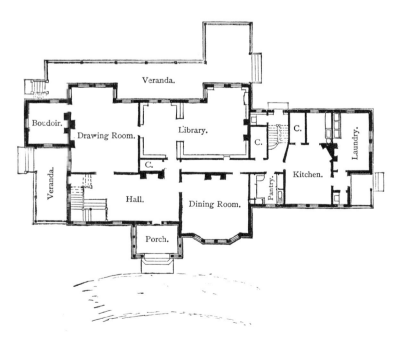

14. Charles T. Cook residence, Elberon, N.J.; McKim, Mead & White, architects, 1885. Elberon's first major season began in 1877, when the Elberon Hotel opened and 20 surrounding cottages were rented. Early cottagers envisioned a resort which would vie "in quietness, gentility, and perhaps exclusiveness with Newport and the other high-toned watering places." During the 1880s the importance of the hotel declined and the center of social life shifted to the new private homes built along Ocean Avenue. Elberon never became a serious threat to those "high-toned" coastal resorts. However, its orderliness and moderate high fashion clearly distinguished it from the excursion atmosphere of Long Branch, immediately to the north. Begun in 1884, this house was completed a year later at a cost of approximately $33,000. Its partially symmetrical composition of two towers connected by a recessed central section was atypical of elevations in this series. A plausible but unsubstantiated explanation of the double nature of the house was that Cook, president of Tiffany and Co., was the best of friends with Charles Tiffany, the company's founder and father of the stained-glass designer Louis Tiffany. Because they spent their leisure time together, Cook asked the architects to create a house in which the two families could fit comfortably. Artistically, this house is far removed from those picturesque, asymmetrical and well-textured houses intimately set in the timbered hills or promontories of Manchester-by-the-Sea or Bar Harbor. In part, this difference may be explained by the relatively treeless and flat expanse of Elberon in the 1880s. Probably more significant was the mid-decade inclination of McKim, Mead & White toward increasing order and sobriety in both plans and elevations. Compared to their earlier work, such as the Goelet house (plates 4 and 5) and the Newport Casino (plates 16 and 17), this house is cooler in color and mood; its walls, despite the shingles, appear thinner and flatter, and the main facade seems more evenly composed and deliberately stated. The design implies tendencies that are not fulfilled because they are checked by competing tendencies. For example, the impression that the elevation is shaped by expanding pressures within is contradicted by the conclusion that some sec-

tions of the wall look static and the ornament stuck on. Unsure of whether the appearance of the house results from internal necessities or arbitrary cosmetic acts, we debate whether to call it studiously casual or expressively refined. While the plan is open, it is also influenced by the obvious concerns for symmetry in the parlor and dining room and also in the large hall (29′ × 24′). The west tower (right) and part of the central section remain at 20 Lincoln Avenue, but the shingles have been covered by white stucco. The double porch of the Atlantic side has been replaced by a one-story Mediterranean-style block.

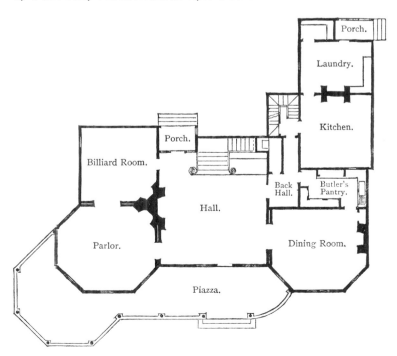

15. "Homestead," Julia Appleton residence, Lenox, Mass.; McKim, Mead & White, architects, 1884. When Sheldon remarked that "undoubtedly the private residence in Lenox, Massachusets, which of late has caused most discussion and awakened the greatest interest is that of Miss Julia Appleton," he was probably referring to the local fascination with its semi-octagonal court, ostensibly to preserve an elm tree, and to its "Old Colonial" flavor. While agreeing, Sheldon also liked "Homestead" because it was modern without being skittish or naïve like some Queen Anne houses, and because it lacked the bucolic casualness of many simpler shingle houses. Here was an intriguing summer residence, progressive in form, pace and comfort but sophisticated and even learned in style. However, the motives and implications of the house were complex. The argument that protecting the tree determined the plan is weakened by the knowledge that the property was large, large enough to be laid out by F. L. Olmsted. If the tree were so important, why was there only one window—in the sitting room—from which it could be seen from the family side of the first floor? The court side of the house chaperoned the Appleton sisters; the other side, with its triple windows and projections, treated them like nature-loving adults. An angle-shaped plan was not unique in the early 1880s; Sheldon included examples of such planning by Dodd (plate 29), Rotch and Tilden (plate 31), Peabody and Stearns (plate 39), Emerson (plate 51), Price (plate 65), a second McKim, Mead & White (plate 83), Little (plate 88), Sturgis and Brigham (plate 92) and Allen and Kenway (plate 96). Basically, these architects reserved the angled extension for servants and entrances, but in this plan the principal rooms, normally protected in the core of the house, were pushed out to the end. The box was broken, so much so that the back stairs faced the front. Paradoxically, this spatially adventurous interior was contained by eighteenth-century brown clapboards and delicate white ornament. Scully's insight is helpful: "It was probably White who consciously, perhaps even ironically exploited and exaggerated the applied character that such Colonial details had always possessed, tending to look as if they could be sliced off with a razor." The house, which cost $20,643, was not small; the cornice of the wing was 23' high and that of the central and right sections 25' high. The smallest of the rooms, the sitting or writing room, measured 15' × 16'. "Homestead," no longer standing, was commissioned by Julia and Alice Appleton, daughters of Charles Appleton of Boston. McKim met Julia in May of 1883 and married her in June 1885. She died in January 1887, and the estate was sold two years later. The proceeds from the sale were divided into three bequests: to the Boston Lying-In Hospital, which she had supported, and to Columbia and Harvard Universities for traveling scholarships in architecture.

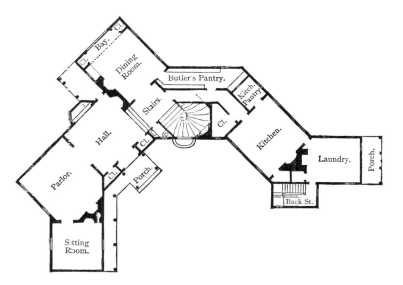

16 and 17. Newport Casino, Newport, R.I.; McKim, Mead & White, architects, 1880. James Gordon Bennett, Jr. (1841–1918), the son of the founder and editor of the New York *Herald*, on which he succeeded his father, and founder of the *Evening Telegram* in New York, was the force behind the Casino at Newport. According to one tale, he decided to form a new club when he became angry at his old one, the Reading Room, for denying privileges to one of his British friends who rode a horse into the building on a dare. In an inclusive frame of mind, he argued successfully with his fellow backers for a low entrance fee that would enable nonmembers to enter the grounds. In theory, poor and rich alike could sit on the piazzas. "The poor mechanic or clerk can take his wife and children to the Casino every Sunday night and listen to a capital concert for 25 cents per head and only twice that amount is charged for admission in the daytime," reported the *Times* in 1886. If Bennett had not been affronted, another spark would probably have activated some Newport regular to call for such a gathering place. Within a few years of its completion in 1880, at a cost of $64,000, cottagers and townspeople were saying that they did not know how they had survived without it. The Casino at Newport probably was the first and best known of its architectural genre. Why did Sheldon include it and three others—the casinos at Narragansett Pier (plate 52), Short Hills (plate 26) and Elberon (plate 78)—in *Artistic Country-Seats*? Possibly because they were designed by architects who designed many houses within the series, because visually they reflected contemporary domestic trends and because they were the social focuses of the owners of the suburban and resort seats he included. Built by a prestigious firm at a prestigious place in a distinctive manner that elevated its vernacular qualities to a place of honor

in late nineteenth-century architecture, the Casino has been one of the most frequently discussed American buildings of the last 100 years. Shortly after it was completed, Mariana van Rensselaer understood that it suited its time and purpose uniquely. "If the gay world at Newport had built itself a Casino some twenty or even ten years ago, I wonder what we should have had? Possibly an imitation of the formal, stately, classicized *Kurhaus* of some German bath. Perhaps a cousin of those fantastically hideous travesties of Oriental pleasure-houses which we find in so many small foreign watering-places. More probably still, a 'Queen Anne' structure which would have looked like an agglomerate of English model-almshouses. At all events, it is safe to say we should not have had anything so sensible yet novel, so simple yet picturesque, so useful yet charming, as Messrs. McKim, Mead and White have given us. The problem was a new one in many respects, both as to the practical ends that were proposed and as to the general expression and sentiment that were desirable to bring the building into harmony with the place itself and with the life whose central point it forms. And the architects were fortunately inspired to set their own wits to work and find a new solution based on common sense and a feeling for beauty, and not on precedent or formula. In its general expression the building is, I think, very adequate and characteristic. It is dignified enough without being formal or pretentious; rural, but not rustic; graceful, intimate, cheerful, with just a touch of fantasy not out of place in a structure whose ends are distinctly frivolous—a Casino which is a mere summer-house for 'society's' amusement." The entrance into the central court, approximately 170′ × 115′, is located in the middle of a row of shops collected under a bilaterally symmetrical facade of gables on Bellevue Avenue. This courtyard, electrically illuminated in

1886, was a great lawn with a fountain at the east end and a U-shaped pathway used for promenading. To the left as one entered the court was a fat tower, the most convincing evidence of the fantasy van Rensselaer referred to, which rose about 60′ and contained the office of the Executive Committee of the Casino. Continuing to the left, the north side held the café and restaurant and, on the second floor, an open piazza now destroyed by fire. The main artery of the Casino, however, was the wide, airy, light and sensitively screened piazza. Here the designers created a reassuring architecture of movement, openness and delicacy, intimate enough for private conversation or contemplation and public enough to serve traffic and to enable those within to survey those without. Beyond the single-story, semicircular piazza were the famed tennis courts. Lawn tennis was introduced to Newport in 1875, shortly after its laws had been codified in England. With fashionable society turning out to see the matches, the Newport tournament in August was for years one of the most important in the country. Today the south piazza has been transformed into the National Lawn Tennis Hall of Fame and a tennis court occupies the central yard.

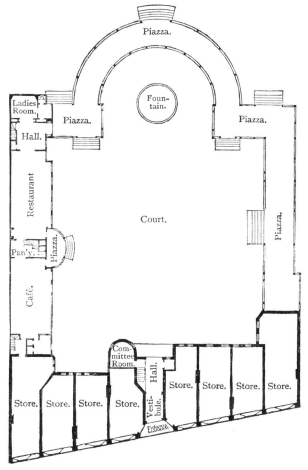

18. Herter residence, Monmouth Beach, N.J.; William B. Bigelow, architect, 1881. Families have wanted to live near the sea because they have been fascinated by it—because they wanted to see it, to listen to it and to smell and feel its breezes. However, both clients and architects have often underestimated its mobility and destructive force. The area between the sea and Ocean Avenue, which connected Sea Bright and Elberon, was lined with hotels and summer mansions a century ago, but storms and eroding beaches have combined to eliminate much of the spectacular architecture of this resort strip. Built upon the sand, the Herter house no longer stands; its site is now under water. Although Sheldon claimed the house was erected in 1879, the decorative panel of the porch, possibly a later addition, carried the date of 1881. The basement story was made of brick, the northern end of the lower floors of brick and cement panels, and the remainder covered with shingles and clapboards. Bigelow created an odd, two-layered exterior: a trim shingle-style house above and a disunified base composed of the planar walls of cement and paneling on the north and the picturesque veranda to the south. The plants and flowers for which houses along this coast were famous partially obscured the high basement common in the region. Since the house was approximately 75′ in length, the surrounding veranda, 9′ to 15′ in width, was probably 175′ long. Within, the largest room was the dining room (18′ × 30′). The plan was unusual in several respects. It rejected the usual importance of the approach to the piazza and similarly squeezed the vestibule between the hall stairway and the butler's pantry, which, with the stairs to the basement kitchen, was not marked. Since the bedroom and studio were family spaces and the hall a traffic area, only the dining room

and parlor were available for guests. Strange then that the exit from the bedroom, a rarity on the main floor, led into this parlor. This peculiarity may be explained by the possibly deteriorating health of the probable owner, Christian Herter (1840–1883), the leading designer of the famed Herter Brothers of New York, furniture makers and interior decorators. Conceivably, the painting studio and bedroom were included on the main floor because Herter, who died two years after the house was completed, may have been physically limited when the house was planned. Finished in pine, its cost was a modest $12,000. Bigelow was a partner with McKim and Mead in 1878 but left the firm to establish a private practice the following year. He retired in 1899.

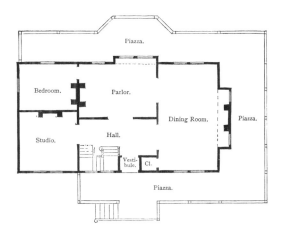

19. "Seaverge," George F. Baker residence, Monmouth Beach, N.J.; Bruce Price, architect, ca. 1884. Sheldon mentioned the "solid" look and "distinctive effect" of this house but was unable to categorize its particular appearance. He concluded that it was not classic, Gothic or Renaissance. Price (1845–1903) created a strong elevation for a house on the beach. While the second story was systematically composed and held together by the texture of Akron tiles, not shingles as we might assume, the first was broken into sections. Those to the left were solidly built of Haverstraw brick. To the right the sections became the voids of the loggia and porte-cochere outlined by the arbitrary rustication and milk-bottle columns. Despite these sections, intended to make the lower story more visually compelling, the second story, for a seaside cottage, was surprisingly reserved. Atypically, the public side was asymmetrical and the facade facing the sea much less so. The design recognized the importance of comings and goings at summer and vacation houses, a responsibility Price addressed in a 1893 article in *Scribner's Magazine*: "Plan and place the house upon its site so that the approach and entrance door shall be upon one side and the lawn and living rooms upon the opposite. Stating it directly, the best work enables us to approach by a drive upon one side, alight at an entrance porch, enter by an entrance-hall, advance thence into the hall, and through it out upon the veranda, and so on upon the lawn." Particularly during the 1880s, Price's planning was distinctive. The Baker house was one of the few in this series without a living room or a parlor and was also a rare case of a plan in which the library was the central space. Price also rejected the normal practice of placing the back stairs in the rear of the house. These steps led to the basement where the kitchen was located, an arrangement that was common for large houses of the Long Branch area built along the ocean. Erected two lots south of Mrs.

Herter's house (plate 18), it has been destroyed by the receding of the shoreline. Artistically inventive, Price was socially conservative. Charming, attractive and respected, he met clients at the posh clubs of New York City, where he established a practice in 1877, at Bar Harbor and at Tuxedo Park. George Baker, associated with the First National Bank and with the Astor Bank of New York, was considered one of the wealthiest men of the country when he died in 1931. He gave Columbia University its stadium and Dartmouth its library. He owned "Seaverge" until 1901 when he moved his country address to Tuxedo Park, that remarkable community financed by Pierre Lorillard and designed by Bruce Price.

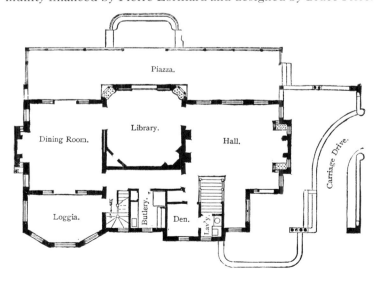

20. "Maybrook," Henry C. Gibson residence, Wynnewood, Pa.; G. W. and W. D. Hewitt, architects, 1881. George Watson Hewitt (1841–1916) and his brother William D. Hewitt (1848–1924) formed a successful partnership in Philadelphia from 1877 to 1902. Designers of the Bourse and Bellevue-Stratford hotel of that city, over 50 churches, usually in the Victorian Gothic style, and many secular buildings in a variety of conservative revival styles, their plans tended to be somewhat simpler than their massive and sometimes coarse exteriors. This generalization is applicable to the Gibson house, constructed of buff sandstone from Plainfield, N.J. and covered with red Vermont slate. Its appearance reminds one of the Houston (plate 70), Clothier (plate 42), Benson (plate 40), Brown (plate 38) and Simpson (plate 35) houses which Sheldon also selected from the western parts and suburbs of Philadelphia. Like them this residence was expensive, large, high (its tower rising 72′), asymmetrical and picturesque in skyline, and artistically inspired by earlier periods that were often highly romanticized but not well understood. What was the intended message of this kind of domestic architecture? Possibly its scale expressed the abundant resources of the family within, its skyline pride and vigor, and its historical references knowledge, good taste and a desired association with the proven past rather than the unpredictable present even though the present made the house possible in the first place. New wealth did not mind old containers, a truism demonstrated on European soil centuries before the idea crossed the Atlantic. On the other hand, they were not old containers, for repeating the past would have been impractical, a criticism a successful businessman would not have appreciated. They were usually creative marriages of forms inspired by the past with materials and purposes conditioned by the present. Sheldon reported that there was not "a square foot of exposed wood-work" and that, consequently, Gibson had not spent a cent on repairs of any kind. Two hot-air furnaces were located in the basement and in the attic were two lead water tanks, filled by steam pumps, which controlled the sanitary system of the house. Although it was one of the longest houses in the series (even its stable was under the same roof), its major rooms, roughly 24′ × 18′, were not unduly large for Philadelphia suburban mansions. The quality of the finish, however, was exceptional. All of the floors were oak, except the hall, which was laid in German tile; the woodwork of the hall was oak, of the parlor walnut, the library butternut, and the dining room mahogany. Although his principal residence was on Walnut Street, Gibson (d. 1891), a Philadelphia distiller, decorated "Maybrook" with numerous objects and paintings from his impressive art collection. The house still stands on Penn Road.

**21. Samuel Colman residence, Newport, R.I.; McKim, Mead &
White, architects, 1883.** Colman was a successful landscape
painter and decorator who was born in Portland, Me. in 1832 and
died in New York City in 1920. A pupil of Asher B. Durand, he
continued his education in Europe from 1860 to 1862 and from
1871 until 1876. He was one of the founders of the American Water
Color Society and in 1866 became its first president. In 1879 he
joined Louis Comfort Tiffany and others in forming Associated
Artists, a firm that specialized in finishing the interiors of large
urban houses. His particular areas of responsibility were fabrics,
wallpapers and ceiling papers. A survey of his house provides us
with some insights into the personal environment of one of the
known artists of the day. If artists could afford a second home,
they usually avoided the popular resorts. Colman disregarded this,
as he also ignored the conventional wisdom that "a man cannot
serve two masters, and an artist, be he never so genial, cannot
give himself to polo, lawn-tennis, garden parties, and society, and
be worthy of his calling." His studio was located in a wide dormer
between the second and third floors on the opposite side of this
elevation. Its ceiling was high, and the lighting excellent. On a
mantel framed by columns was the artistic focal point of the studio:
an arrangement of individual pieces of a complete set of Japanese
armor. After considerable experimentation in the hall, he finally
stained its oak wainscoting and ceiling a neutral tint to prevent
the wood from looking either too red or too green when it darkened. Following popular taste, he covered the walls of the hall
with Japanese leather paper, a material that could be cleaned
easily. For accents he chose an olive Persian jar, a Japanese chest
and Japanese bronzes. Including objects from different cultures
was acceptable if they could be combined harmoniously. Furthermore, worldwide bric-a-brac announced the breadth of one's
cultural experiences. Early in the 1890s Colman presented the

Metropolitan Museum with a collection of his Japanese ceramics.
Decorators often treated each room as an independent unit. In the
library the prevailing color of wood was blue-black, and in the
drawing room the color scheme was rose and buff supported by
similarly colored objects—a buff chair, a rose vase. Although it
was not one of McKim, Mead & White's finest houses of the early
1880s, it was, in the words of Mariana van Rensselaer, "dignified
yet rural, simple yet refined, almost picturesque yet quiet." Furthermore, it was evidence that good architecture did not necessarily require an interior and exterior of like character. If Colman
managed to create an interior atmosphere appropriate for oriental
porcelains and Persian silks, the architects designed an exterior
that looked as if it might have been converted from an old gambrel-
roof barn. Built for approximately $25,000, the house still stands
on Red Cross Avenue.

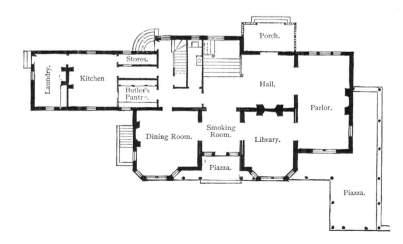

22. "Farwood," Richard L. Ashhurst residence, Overbrook, Pa.; Wilson Eyre, Jr., architect, 1885. This house has been regarded by contemporary critics and later historians as one of Eyre's finest country houses of the 1880s. Though elongated, it is held together, to a large extent, by the cornices of the first and second floors, which seem to sweep rapidly back and forth across the 100'-long facade. Because this side was decisively layered, the height of the gambrel roof did not seem exceptional. On the other side, however, where the ground was lower, this barnlike form stood out boldly, a bulky section that looked too heavy for the lightly framed veranda which cut underneath it. The facade in this photograph, though designed with greater concern for artistic wholeness, contained several distinctive, even peculiar, features. In order to draw attention to the unifying middle level and possibly to mimic the barns of the area, Eyre projected the second floor over the stone walls of the first. In Sheldon's opinion, "the heavy overhangs and the lowness of the structure, together with its length and the number of its gables, are the principal features of all of Mr. Wilson Eyre's suburban cottage work." As a result of this overhang, the first story appeared to be dwarfed and partially in shadow, weakening the invitation to enter the house. In a compensatory mood Eyre identified the doorway with cascading parentheses and ornamented the walls of the first floor with an odd assortment of window openings. A less skillful architect probably would have combined the disparate materials of the exterior—gray stone, shingles in wave courses and pebble-dash panels between the timbers—without this impression of natural randomness. The plan of the first floor was one of the simplest and also one of the most

tightly integrated of this series. Three rooms formed one space, the direction of which was reinforced by the open and well-lighted veranda. Several steps led down to the lower hall where placed highlights were immediately evident: wide windows and a fine vista directly ahead, a massive fireplace slightly to the left, and, to the right and left, respectively, the recessed fireplace of the dining room and octagonal bay of the drawing room. Wood was effectively introduced in the complicated stairway and the arch that framed the dining-room mantel. "Farwood" has been demolished. Ashhurst maintained a residence on South 11th Street in Philadelphia in addition to this country house. Born in 1838, he was admitted to the bar in 1859, became active in Philadelphia's social life, and was appointed for two terms as postmaster of the city. He died mysteriously in 1911 when he apparently fell into the ocean from a pier at Atlantic City.

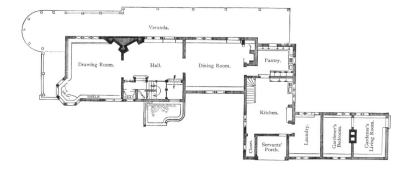

23. Charles A. Newhall residence, Philadelphia, Pa.; Wilson Eyre, Jr., architect, ca. 1881. The domestic architecture of Eyre in the 1880s was influenced by the houses of British architect Richard Norman Shaw (1831–1912). In the Newhall house the Shavian reminders were the overhangs, half-timbered sections, banks of windows, casements, horizontal roof lines and artistic groupings. The two architects often employed sturdy materials for the first story and more picturesque materials above. However, the shingled and half-timbered surfaces of Eyre's houses, by comparison, seem more eclectic and nervous and decidedly thinner. Shaw designed masses, Eyre bounded volumes with interrupted planes. Although the varied forms, textures, materials (stone quarried in Germantown, brick, paneling, shingles and cypress shingles on the roof) and moods of these facades could be considered creative explications of a basic concept, they could also be interpreted as signs of compositional searching. The differences between Shaw and Eyre were more apparent in their plans, for the former organized additively while the latter, in the words of Vincent Scully, demonstrated a marked "sense of axial discipline, of spatial interpenetration, and of horizontal continuity." The plan of the Newhall residence was less a mosaic of visual effects—a judgment that could be made of the exterior—than a concentrated effort to heighten one's awareness and delight of space. From this side of the house the experience of entering was conditioned by the hardness and right-angled turns of the lower terrace and its narrow stairway. Eyre sustained this sense of constriction to the foot of the stairs where, suddenly, the openness of the hall became apparent. He used the same device in the Ashhurst house (plate 22), but the space of the Newhall house was more demanding and compelling. It was more complicated because the stairway of double landings led to a two-floor gallery that extended around three sides of the hall. Consequently, the hall was significant vertically as well as horizontally. By placing fireplaces and seats cleverly in adjacent spaces of the main floor, Eyre lured the curious into these surrounding rooms, inviting them to realize the nature of the interior through a series of intimate discoveries in addition to their initial grand impression reached in the hall. The pine woodwork was stained with unusual colors: a virtual black for the hall, dark red for the parlor and library, and bronze for the dining room. The elongated plan permitted direct access to the porch on the opposite side of the hall and enabled servants to function without impinging on social space. Furthermore, the buffer of the back hall, laundry and closet reduced noise and odors emanating from the large, bright kitchen. Now demolished, this $13,000 Chestnut Hill house was approximately 100′ long and, in the family section, 30′ wide.

24. J. H. Van Alen residence, Newport, R.I.; Clarence S. Luce, architect, n.d. When Clarence Luce died in 1924 at the age of 73, he was a reasonably well-known architect, although architectural historians subsequently have paid him little attention. Recognized for his Massachusetts State Building at the Philadelphia Centennial, he designed structures for later exhibitions at St. Louis, Jamestown, Portland and Paris. The majority of his nonexposition work was done in the New York and Washington areas. Like the Josephs house (plate 11) he designed at Middletown, R.I., the Van Alen residence was long (150′), narrow (40′) and dominated by a gambrel roof. Unlike the disciplined and restrained expression of the Josephs house, this was exuberantly baroque in character, a festival of dormers, bays, Elizabethan gables, buttressed chimneys and balconies. Here he exaggerated and itemized the parts, in the Josephs house he simplified and subordinated them. Starting in the middle of the 1880s, *The Builder* of London noted with enthusiasm the increasing quality and distinctiveness of American houses, but when its editors published an illustration of the Van Alen house in December 1886, they identified it as one still dependent on English prototypes. If the owner had read this, he would have been pleased, because he was a dedicated Anglophile. A general in the Civil War, he spent much of his life in Europe, particularly in Britain. For the hall of the main floor he imported an early English oak mantel consisting of carved hunting scenes and grotesque figures supporting the shelf. Another artistic highlight were the landing's stained-glass windows which, as we can see, occupied an unusually large amount of wall space and on a sunny day bathed the staircase with reds, yellows and blues. The dimensions of the library were 16′ × 18′ and the vast, T-shaped drawing room consumed almost 1,000 square feet. Judging from the location of the children's dining room, a rarity at this time, youngsters were expected to be neither seen nor heard. Another rarity was the European custom of sheltering animals and humans under the same roof. Costing approximately $13,000, a surprisingly low price for a house of these measurements in this area, the exterior was finished in brick and shingles and the woodwork was stained ash. Van Alen's house no longer exists but the home he built on his property for his son, James J., is still standing on Ochre Point Avenue. Called "Wakehurst" and erected between 1882 and 1888 by Dudley Newton, who copied the garden front of Wakehurst Place, Sussex, this second house was given to his son to console him for the death of his wife, the daughter of William Astor, at the age of 28. The garage of "Wakehurst" was erected on the site of the house in this photograph.

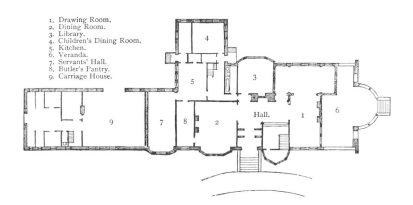

1. Drawing Room.
2. Dining Room.
3. Library.
4. Children's Dining Room.
5. Kitchen.
6. Veranda.
7. Servants' Hall.
8. Butler's Pantry.
9. Carriage House.

25. Joseph T. Low residence, Seabright, N.J.; Arthur B. Jennings, architect, 1885. After graduating from the City College of New York in 1870, Arthur Bates Jennings (1849–1927) trained in the offices of George B. Post and Russell Sturgis. Although better known for his church and educational architecture, he designed houses early in his career and built a large number on New York's Upper West Side. He received commissions for educational buildings from Oberlin College, Washington and Jefferson College and Fordham University. During the 1890s Jennings built numerous Protestant churches, most of them in a modified modern Romanesque style with a single tower located at the right angle of two wings. The picturesque skylines of these churches in stone are reminiscent of the animated skylines of his earlier domestic work in wood. The Low house illustrated a truism of architecture, that the setting could encourage a degree of license in design and planning that probably would be condemned in another location. The architect's responsibility here was to shape a suitably large summer home for a New York family that would be impressive enough to reflect the client's social and economic status and also express the informality, openness and liveliness of life at the beach. The house had to look as if it could protect the family within and, at the same time, enable the vacationers to engage the world outside. The steep roofs of the high gables and the broad chimneys identify the sheltering core of the house; the sleeping porches, tower and veranda recognize the importance of places in the house where the sun and air could be enjoyed. Jennings further explained the character of the house through the unabashedly picturesque and spatially intricate attic level and roof. The peaks build to a crescendo in the high tower, the whole ensemble announcing the expected festive and playful life at the seashore. Jennings probably devised the plan to support the appearance he wanted, for, unlike the exterior, the plan lacks a central idea. With the exception of the billiard room and parlor, these rooms tend to function independently of one another. The Long Branch area of the Jersey coast eventually became a Philadelphia summer colony, but in these years, as this series verifies, prominent New Yorkers built cottages from Seabright on the north to Elberon on the south. Low, born in Louisville, Ky. in 1846, moved to New York where he founded Low, Harriman and Company and, in 1886, Joseph T. Low and Company, which represented several major dry-goods factories. Erected at the corner of Rumson Road and the Avenue of the Two Rivers, the structure has been demolished.

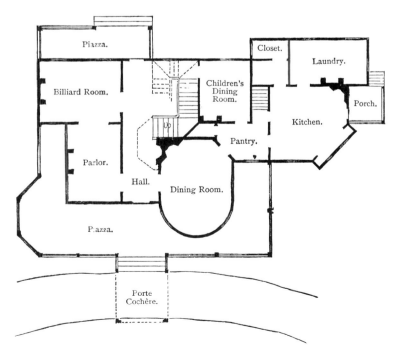

26. Short Hills Casino, Short Hills, N.J.; McKim, Mead & White, architects, 1880. Short Hills was the result of Stewart Hartshorn's long-standing dream of building an ideal community. Financing the project through money from a window-blind patent, he bought land in the 1870s near Millburn, N.J., created a road system, laid the sewer and water pipes, and found architects to design modest houses that would blend with the superb natural setting. Over fifty families had settled in Short Hills by 1888. According to Leland Roth, Hartshorn commissioned McKim, Mead & White in 1879 to design a small house and a casino or music hall. White, who had just joined the firm, designed the latter. The Casino was used not only as a clubhouse for artistic and social events but also as the village's first school, for several years as the meeting place of the Episcopalian congregation and for several decades as town hall. The contemporaneous response of architectural critics to Short Hills was mixed. Hartshorn had succeeded in materializing his dream so well that some observers objected to its storybook appearance. For example, an article in the July, 1884 issue of *Lippincott's Magazine* praised White's skill in relieving the potential monotony of this barn-like structure with a "portly round tower," in turn relieving the monotony of the tower with an attached chimney stack of rough stone, barely visible in this photograph, and sustaining the rustic appearance throughout by using rock-face stone in the basement, rough brick in the openings and chimneys, and black slate in the tower and roof. But he questioned the combination of rustic elements and "starveling and stringy classicized detail." More serious, he thought, was White's quest for expression at the expense of purpose. "But when one moves the previous question why a round tower should be crowned with a square roof, the building does not yield an answer, and the roof begins to look very irrelevant to the tower which it crowns, and the tower to the building of which it relieves the monotony. It is an example of that kind of design in which the 'effect' precedes the cause..." In retrospect White's exterior seems as delightful as it is contrived. If he erred in overdressing a simple structure, he

created within it a functional auditorium, stage and supporting rooms. This interior, like the village itself, was technologically up-to-date; steam pipes were hidden under the built-in seats of the auditorium walls, and gas fixtures were included during construction. Built for only $9,000, the building lasted until February, 1978 when it was destroyed by fire. For the last five decades of its existence, it was known as the Racquets Club.

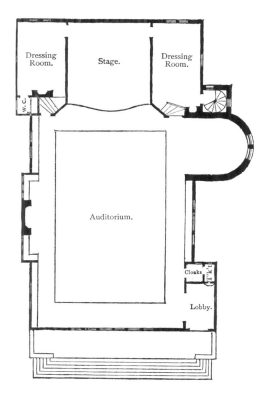

27. Henry P. Talmadge residence, Plainfield, N.J.; Douglas Smythe, architect, n.d. Knowing that the owners of these houses were the individuals who would purchase copies of the limited edition of *Artistic Country-Seats*, Sheldon attempted to comment positively on the examples he chose. He may have anticipated a skeptical response from some readers for including the flamboyant Talmadge mansion for he prefaced his judgment, a "beautiful house," with a paragraph denying a current charge that American architects were merely satisfying their desire for exotic effects. He thus revealed his political savvy rather than his artistic judgment. As a design that stimulated the imagination, however, it was superb. Surprisingly, this house was commissioned by a social and economic conservative, the head of Henry Talmadge & Co., a respected New York banking firm, who was also a director of the Central Trust Co. and the Mechanics National Bank. Why did Talmadge approve a design so unlike the sober nature of his professional life? Possibly he subscribed to the notion that city residences should be discreet but those in the country could be spirited. Possibly he reasoned that his successes deserved a massive spatial and material demonstration. Costing $45,000, 92' long, 62' wide and rising 48' to the tower balcony, the house was not expressed apologetically. Instead of faulting client and architect for their indiscretion, we should first recognize our restricted vision, shaped, as Steven McQuillin has put it, by the "bastardized colonial and cheap, ineffectual Tudor that middle class America lives in today." Also, too many architectural historians, influenced by Scully's invaluable *The Shingle Style*, have unfortunately divided the suburban architecture of the 1880s into the progressive and the unenlightened, forgetting that the latter is an equally important conduit for understanding history. Smythe (sometimes spelled Smyth), an architect of New York City, used brick, Belle-

ville stone and shingles for the exterior. The tower, servants' veranda and two-story family veranda offered fine views of the valley and mountains to the west. Because of the slope, the west wall of the basement was above ground; it contained the kitchen, laundry, wine cellar, storeroom and furnace room. The hall was exceptionally large (25' × 38'), as was the library (18' × 32'), but the other rooms—billiard room (24' × 18'), dining room (16' × 25') and parlor (18' × 20')—were often this size in large houses. The hall was finished in antique oak while the other rooms of the first floor were done in either ash or cherry. The Talmadge house was destroyed by fire in 1969.

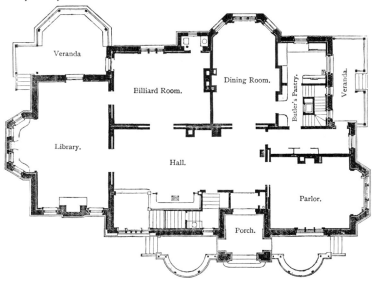

28. Charles W. McCutchen residence, North Plainfield, N.J.; Charles H. Smith, architect, n.d. In the mid-1880s the McCutchen house was thought to be one of the outstanding examples of contemporary domestic architecture in Plainfield. It was solid and reassuring, an impression conveyed primarily by the relatively uninterrupted surfaces of the main roofs, the clean horizontal lines of the veranda roof, and the two blocky sections of the house which intersect at right angles. On the other hand, to insure that this appearance of solidity did not mean a dull design, Smith, a little-known architect of New York City, included several unusual elements and combinations of elements on the main facade. He linked the almost colorless stained-glass window, exceptionally large (19′ × 7′) for a house of this size, with the two windows to the right by means of a peculiar pathway of masonry. Less unusual but by no means common was the window within the widened chimney which Smith intentionally contrasted to the adjacent rect angular window. He also contrasted the playful arched screens of the balcony with the ponderous arch of the main porch. The plan, likewise, was distinctive, though art and utility were not well integrated on the first floor. People standing in the vestibule enjoyed an unbroken view of the windows on the other side of the hall only because the stairway and the main fireplace were pushed to the side and placed unpleasantly close to one another. Visitors entering from the carriage porch came through the dining room or the butler's pantry. To improve the quality of life for the McCutchens, Smith included a Jackson ventilating grate designed to circulate fresh air instead of rewarming stale air, insisted that the plumbing throughout the house be exposed to make the detection of leaks and repairs simpler, and covered the walls around all sinks with tiles. The odors of dirty laundry bothered this generation, not only in the United States but also abroad. At a meeting of the Royal Institute of British Architects in 1898, the aging authority on domestic architecture, Professor Robert Kerr, declared that the built-in closet was one of the most objectionable features of American houses. The closet "would not do in England in any decent house at all; it would get stuffy and altogether nasty from things stowed away there." Concerned about the same condition, Smith built a ventilated dirty-clothes closet beside the bathroom. Its doors were louvered and inside was a sizable exhaust pipe that extended to the highest point of the roof. Located at 21 Rockview Avenue, the house serves today as the Margaret McCutchen Boarding and Nursing Home. McCutchen (1845–1930) was constantly involved in Plainfield's business, religious and civic activities. He was a partner of Holt and Company, export flour merchants in New York City, and was director of numerous banks, including the Corn Exchange Bank.

29. William Pratt residence, Manchester-by-the-Sea, Mass.; Arthur Hooper Dodd, architect, 1883. This fine exterior, a delicate yet lively demonstration of shingles continuously binding curved and angled volumes, probably deserves more attention from historians than it has received. Scully was an exception when he noted similarities between it and its neighbor "Kragsyde" (plate 39) in *The Shingle Style*, although he did not illustrate it. Lack of information has undoubtedly affected the quiet press the Pratt house has received; today we know relatively little about its architect, owner or the reasons for its brief existence. Although Dodd (d. 1901) studied abroad and at M.I.T., he was not a full-time designer, for his inherited income permitted him time to travel and sketch, and in the last years of his life he was better known in Boston for his newspaper articles than for his buildings. Though Pratt (1834–1893) was reported to have sailed the world and served as a captain in the Civil War, his business and professional activities are not well documented. Begun in December 1882, work on his Lobster Cove house was finished about May of 1883. Since Wheaton Holdon has indicated that "Kragsyde," erected on higher adjacent land, was designed and built during 1883–84, it is possible that the angled plan by Peabody and Stearns may have been influenced by the plan of Pratt's cottage. George N. Black, the very wealthy owner of "Kragsyde," objecting to his neighbor's house, purchased Pratt's property and had Dodd's masterpiece summarily torn down in 1892. If Black deserves an orchid for financing the stunning design by Peabody and Stearns, he deserves an onion for such unwarranted destruction. According to local tales, he resented its proximity, yet the lower Pratt house did not block his ocean view. Perhaps his reaction was analogous to that of a party-goer who sees another wearing the same designer original. Like the pastels of Degas, Dodd's exterior expressed a distinctive late nineteenth-century awareness of movement and vibration. Its planes were constantly interrupted or were turned gracefully into new directions. Entasis and re-entrant curves encouraged this impression of fluidity. Furthermore, the surface shimmered, not only the shingles but also the screen that blocked an earlier servants' entrance. The major chimney, blocky below but completed in smoothly laid brick, illustrated in its transition how Dodd turned a physical event into a visual one. Despite extensive blasting to compensate for the 11' difference in levels, the house cost only $11,000. The dramatic dining room was 14' × 21', but the reception room (13' × 14'), hall (14' × 20') and drawing room (14' × 17') formed a quieter unit. The entire first story, including the staircase, was finished in cherry, and the second in stained pine.

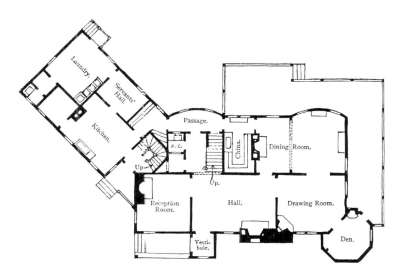

30. "Villa Zorayda," Franklin W. Smith residence, St. Augustine, Fla.; Franklin W. Smith, architect, 1883. Sheldon called this "the most unique private residence in the country." There were good reasons for his conclusion. Franklin W. Smith (the W. stood sometimes for Waldo and sometimes for Webster; 1826–1911) was a wealthy Boston businessman who traveled extensively, was fascinated by ancient and exotic cultures and, with late nineteenth-century enthusiasm for "authentic" recreation as an educational device, constructed historic buildings and rooms on American soil. But he was not an architect. In 1890 he opened his replica of the Pompeian House of Pansa at Saratoga Springs and in 1899 unveiled the Halls of the Ancients on New York Avenue in Washington, D.C. While in Spain in 1882, Smith decided to build a winter home in St. Augustine. "Villa Zorayda," named for the second of three princesses in Washington Irving's "The Alhambra," initiated a fad for Moorish architecture in that city in the 1880s and early 1890s. Because Iberian architecture was not constructed of wood, and stone was not available in Florida, Smith used Portland cement plus coquina. This mixture, strengthened by the calcium of the shells, was poured into molds made of 10″ planks. Because this system required that the previous level harden before a new level could be poured, the building, even today, appears to have been built of elongated concrete blocks. The foundation, walls, chimney and battlements were made of concrete. A description of the interior was published in a local paper in March, 1900: "The two-storied galleries surround the entire court, supported by graceful horseshoe arches reinforced by iron rods, which are covered over, as are the walls of the court, with delicate traceries in which are reproduced numberless quotations from the Koran. These arabesques are exact copies from the walls of the Alhambra. The Spanish tiles forming the dado are from Valencia. The balustrade is copied from one in Cairo. The ancient weapons hanging on the walls are from Morocco. The old brasses, from which the visitor is served with Moorish coffee or spiced halvah with Oriental sweets, come from Granada." Smith leased this house at 83 King Street in 1902. Although it is today a museum known as "Zorayda Castle," it looks quite similar (the crenelation of the tower is gone) to the house that Sheldon illustrated. The site history of this property by David Nolan is excellent.

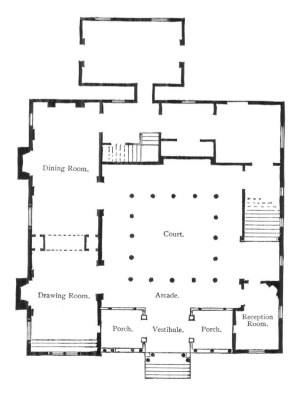

31. "Chatwold," G. B. Bowler residence, Bar Harbor, Me.; Rotch and Tilden, architects, 1883. One of the most popular watering places for New York, Boston, Philadelphia and New Orleans society, Bar Harbor on Mount Desert Island was first discovered by American artists, among them Thomas Cole and Frederick Church, before the middle of the nineteenth century. In the 1880s it attracted the young searching for summer romances and intellectuals content to "walk and talk." Dances at the 500-room Rodicks Hotel, built in 1882, drew 3,000 people twice a week. The mountains, sea and fine air encouraged an athletic and informal social atmosphere. Mrs. Bowler's formidable house contradicts this generalization. Sheldon offered an explanation: "The effort has been to combine the solid attractions of a city home with the less solid attractions of a typical home by the seaside." The house, no longer extant, was illustrated frequently in the mid-1880s. Mariana van Rensselaer praised the color worked into the exterior: rough gray stone of the tower, gray granite walls with red granite trim, dark red timbers separating light plaster sprinkled with red granite pebbles, and dark stained roof shingles. The *Deutsche Bauzeitung* of September, 1887 was less complimentary. Admittedly picturesque, the house, dependent on English forerunners, did not show the expected independence of recent American designers. Despite the strong influence of English half-timber architecture and the conglomeration of elements on the exterior, the plan of "Chatwold" was unified and contemporary. Rotch and Tilden utilized the open planning of central heating brilliantly to create a vista, 80′ long, through four principal rooms. The hall formed the shorter axis and linked the entrance porch with the rear piazza. Moreover, it was important in unifying the house vertically. Number 7 on the plan marked the landing, affording a spectacular view of the sea below through a wide wall of glass and studs. The meeting point of the two legs of the plan separated family space from servant space, the latter identified on the exterior by "inferior" shingles. Arthur Rotch (1850–1894) and George Thomas Tilden (1845–1919) formed their partnership in 1880 after excellent educations in Boston and at the École des Beaux-Arts in Paris. Designers primarily of houses, churches and educational buildings, the firm was not one of the pacesetting offices of the 1880s, and Rotch is probably best remembered today for the scholarship bearing his family's name that has enabled architects under 30 to study abroad.

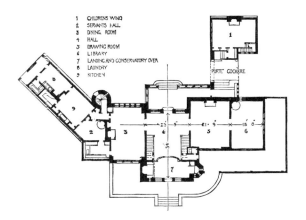

32. "Sunset Hall," Samuel P. Hinckley residence, Lawrence, N.Y.; Lamb and Rich, architects, 1883. A builder in Lawrence, Hinckley created an unusual cluster of houses on his property in the 1880s. Illustrated in the journal *Building* in September, 1888, they were all designed by Lamb and Rich and given names inspired by nature—"Elm Hall," "Sunnyside," "Sunset Hall," "Meadow Bank" and "Briar Hill." Sheldon's comments on "Sunset Hall" are among his most perceptive in *Artistic Country-Seats.* "Mr. Hinckley's house has the fundamental artistic quality of depending for its effect not upon ornament, but upon the body of the edifice itself; not upon the added details, but upon the justness of the proportion.... The most representative architects of the present era aim to find beauty less in added ornament than in such qualities as unity, fitness, and the interdependence of parts." The horizontal movement of this long (114') clapboard and shingle exterior was created, in part, by the low ceilings—the second story was only 8½' and the first slightly higher—the clearly marked layers and the stubby chimneys. Through the diagonal vista that linked the major rooms, Rich echoed the generous sweep of the long facade. He employed several means to emphasize the breadth of the first-floor spaces—beamed ceilings, fireplaces with 6½' openings and 11' mantels, the 7' opening between hall and dining room, the 8'-wide base of the stairway and the broad window seats and built-in divans that he included in every room. The light-weight colonial furniture sustained this low center of gravity and did not inhibit physically or psychologically the horizontal flow of space. Few halls in this series expressed American craftsman-ship in wood and the coziness of its function as a sitting room, or demonstrated the versatility of its central role in fluid space better than the hall of "Sunset Hall." Colors also contributed to the liveliness of both the exterior and the interior. The walls of the second story were highlighted with old gold and Indian red. Several gables were faced with colorful pebbles in plaster. Between the brown-stained beams the ceiling of the hall was peacock blue, the parlor was finished in gold and white, the den in blue and the wainscoting of the dining room painted a Brandon red. Hugo Lamb (1848–1903) and Charles Alonzo Rich (1855–1943) formed their partnership shortly before the Hinckley house was built. Based in New York City, the firm was well known for its larger public buildings, usually designed in robust variations of revival styles, and for its picturesque, if not defiantly expressive, designs for country houses. "Sunset Hall" no longer stands.

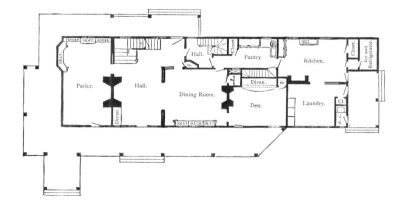

33. "Breakers," Cornelius Vanderbilt residence, Newport, R.I.; Peabody and Stearns, architects, 1877–78. Although it stood for only 14 years, this house was widely known in the nineteenth century and continues to attract the attention of architectural historians today. There are several reasons for this. It was designed by Peabody and Stearns of Boston, whose significant role in these lively years of American architecture has recently been explained and documented by Wheaton Holden. In 1877 Robert Swain Peabody (1845–1917) published influential commentaries in the *American Architect and Building News*, calling to the attention of his colleagues the contemporary importance of both English Queen Anne and American colonial architecture. In this house, which he was designing at that time, he combined picturesque massing, reflecting the Queen Anne, with detail recalling Georgian work of the eighteenth century. However, the composition was not gracefully resolved; the horizontals implied expansion while the vertical members appear to be stiff and pinched. The "Breakers" was also known because of the millionaires who owned it. Pierre Lorillard V, whose family initially was successful in the tobacco business, reportedly paid about $100,000 for the Cliff Walk property and another $90,000 for the original house. After he decided to carry out his scheme for Tuxedo Park, Lorillard sold the house and property in October, 1885 to Cornelius Vanderbilt who then rehired Peabody and Stearns to remodel it because its style was no longer fashionable. Holden uncovered reports from the *Newport Mercury* in December, 1886 explaining that 80 workers had been hired to transform the hall, to replace the finish in several other rooms, and to relocate the kitchen on the northeast side of a new dining room (40′ × 70′), the largest in Newport. The current "Breakers," a fireproof palace in a Ren-

aissance revival mode designed by Richard Morris Hunt, was completed on this site three years after the original structure burned in November, 1892. Even the report of this disaster caused a stir. Defending the quality of their work, Peabody and Stearns charged the *American Architect and Building News* on January 21, 1893 with "making rather free with the facts" in its account of the source of the fire. Obviously, the vast hall was the heart of the plan, and the architects employed the entrance axis to make this clear. However, the double stairway was an act of symmetrical overkill, the proximity of stairs and fireplace meant friction between dissimilar activities, and the fireplace itself looked like a conspicuous single at a couples' dance. The plan was composed of spaces shaped by no controlling principle. Space was used wastefully, and subsidiary rooms—for guns and the toilet, for example—were carved out of what was left over.

34. S. Bayard Dod residence, East Orange, N.J.; Arthur B. Jennings, architect, 1885. This compact yet spatially expressive house stood at 302 S. Harrison Street, south of Central Avenue, until it was demolished in 1941. It cost approximately $20,000. Jennings worked the Newark brownstone, brick and pine shingles into a composition that Sheldon, struggling with its composite nature, defined as "Gothic, particularly in the roof and tower, but this is varied by features of finish which are rather English Gothic, or, to use the ordinary misnomer, Queen Anne." Although Western architects historically have tended to favor designs that look systematic, reasonable and clear, American designers of the 1880s were less predictable. Instead, as the Dod house well illustrates, they frequently created designs marked not by a clearly methodical system but by an apparent randomness. Of course, the house in this photograph was not randomly composed, but the designer knowingly courted this implication, for example, through the ostensibly haphazard manner in which the stone blocks and even the bricks were shaped and laid. The randomness was also expressed by forcing two distinct units, one of stone and one sheathed in shingles, into a plastic conglomerate. The coerced interpenetration of forms, each seeking an independent place in the sun, furthered this impression. Even the sharp drop of the land suggested an accidental rather than a foreordained placement. By taking such chances, Jennings risked the mockery of cooler and more antiseptic tastes, of which the twentieth century has produced its share. The open-minded critic might conclude that he was unable to coordinate his expressive zeal; nevertheless, compared to the timid, cliché-ridden detached houses of recent decades, this one was an affirmation of the notion that the visual dialogue depends upon architecture speaking up. Jennings also deserves credit for trying to make the experience of entering the hall from the front door a memorable one. Immediately ahead was a wide archway, an artistic introduction to the two doors—to the library and the dining room—directly behind it. This trilogy of entrances was distinctive in this series. He also celebrated the act of climbing stairs by placing the first step almost in the center of the hall and by laying the short risers along an octagonal path. Underneath the stairway he installed a window seat while on the entrance side of the staircase he placed a fireplace which Sheldon claimed did not obscure the view of the stairs. Although it suggests a tacked-on family room of the mid-twentieth century, the study was actually a studio, two feet lower than the main floor and illuminated by raised sky-lights, where Dod, an artist, painted. His watercolors decorated the spaces between the panels of the library ceiling.

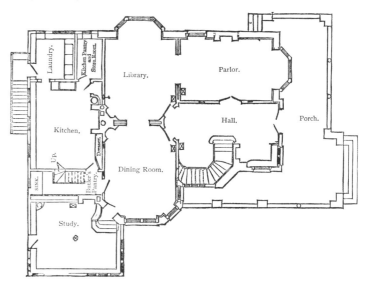

35. "Ingeborg," William Simpson, Jr. residence, Wynnewood, Pa.; Theophilus P. Chandler, Jr., architect, 1884–85. Chandler (1845–1928), settling in Philadelphia about 1871 after study in Italy and a brief practice in Boston, designed at least 124 buildings and projects, most of them between 1876 and 1906. He served as president of the local chapter of the American Institute of Architects for 11 years, beginning in 1888, and was deeply involved in the beginning of the University of Pennsylvania School of Architecture. Nevertheless, Ted Sande, who, with William Bassett, has done much to remind us of Chandler's forgotten importance, has pointed out that his obituaries were short and dry. The *A.I.A. Journal* accorded him three lines. Later historians probably wrote him off because his houses looked stuffy, ponderous and often pretentious. However, his handling of the granite blocks of "Ingeborg" was adroit, for the wall of the north facade, illustrated in the photograph, looked simultaneously carefully and haphazardly laid. Though heavy, the stone barrier was charged with energy by Chandler. He linked windows creatively to brighten the interior or employed them singly to document the rise of interior stairways. This large structure (105′ × 56′) was located at the corner of Lancaster Avenue and Remington Road but has been demolished. It was commissioned by the owner of the internationally known William Simpson Sons & Co., a textile firm. Spacious and carefully finished, the main rooms of the first floor, despite their sliding doors, were meant to be understood primarily as distinct spaces for distinct functions. The hall (24′ × 20′) was finished in oak with wainscoting and a ceiling of open timberwork, the library (16′ × 20′) and dining room (17′ × 32′) were walnut; the parlor (23′ × 23′) and reception room (24′ × 17′) were completed in mahogany. In the conservatory (10′ × 19′) the principal materials were glass and iron. On the second floor were an art gallery, five bedrooms, four bathrooms, and a study, while on the third floor were a billiard room (20′ × 21′), a storeroom (29′ × 19′), four servants' bedrooms, a bathroom and two guest rooms finished in California redwood. Inside shutters were made for all the windows, and the floors were hardwoods. Gas was made on the property by a machine capable of supplying 100 lights. Simpson and Chandler recognized the potential for electricity in the modern house, for they included electric bells, speaking tubes, burglar alarms and telephones, making "Ingeborg" a technically advanced residence for houses of its size and class.

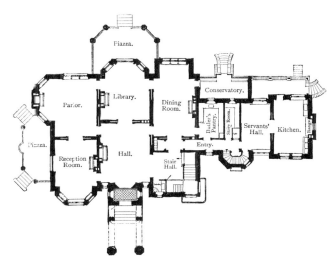

36. Mary F. Stoughton residence, Cambridge, Mass.; Henry H. Richardson, architect, 1883. Mrs. Stoughton's residence, extant at 90 Brattle Street, has been one of the most frequently discussed houses of the late nineteenth century. Henry-Russell Hitchcock wrote, "This is one of his [Richardson's] most successful works and is, perhaps, the best suburban wooden house in America. It is comparable only to the finest of Frank Lloyd Wright's." Vincent Scully concluded, "the Stoughton House, with its spatially expansive living hall and its bulging shingled surfaces was a masterpiece of the new architecture." Sheldon, three years after it was completed, asserted, "few cottages of equal dimensions were ever planned, in this country or abroad, which show better results in point of convenience, spaciousness, and architectural purity." If the large rooms of this open plan exert pressures on the exterior, it was also true that Richardson designed an exterior of integrity, grace and discreet energy and not simply a by-product of the plan. Despite the entrance void and projections above and the juxtaposition of flat and curving walls, the surface of green cypress shingles overrides the separatist tendencies of certain parts. Richardson's concentrated windows tighten the composition and clarify the levels. By restraining the height of the circular cap over the stairway, he reaffirmed in the roof the horizontal orientation of the lower floors. An earlier photograph suggests that the chimney pipes were added later. The curve of the tower was quietly reintroduced in the flaring of the shingle skirt and in the shapes of the entrance loggia and three openings above, which originally contained no glass. This house has also been significant because it was designed by Richardson at the peak of his skill as a domestic architect. Richardson died of Bright's disease in April, 1886, at the moment when the public was acknowledging the "new Renaissance in American architecture" as Sheldon called it, when his

contribution to this Renaissance was verified by a superficial but nevertheless influential 1885 poll conducted by the *American Architect and Building News* to determine the ten best buildings in the United States (five were designed by him), and when Europeans, in the process of discovering American work, were exaggerating his role. Mary Stoughton commissioned the house on the death of her second husband, whose health had failed while serving as ambassador to Russia. An intelligent, artistic woman, she was mother of historian and evolutionist John Fiske by her first marriage. Built as the future "homestead of the Fiske family," the rear of the house was being remodeled and enlarged in 1901 to hold the son's library of some 12,000 volumes when he died suddenly.

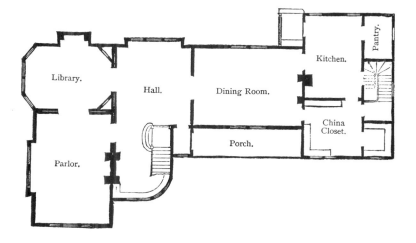

37. "Stonecliffe," Charles Taylor residence, Philadelphia, Pa.; Theophilus P. Chandler, Jr., architect, 1880–81. When this house was illustrated in the *American Architect and Building News* in December, 1882, it was probably owned by T. M. Stewart, who commissioned it ca. 1880. "Stonecliffe" became the residence of Mrs. Charles Taylor some time after April, 1884. Rising high above steeply sloping ground, it was referred to by contemporaries as "remarkably picturesque," and amateur photographers considered the view from its terrace unmatched in Chestnut Hill. Originally, ten acres of land protected its implication of spendid and unthreatened isolation. Chandler got the idea for the terrace from a stone farmhouse he had seen in the suburbs of Philadelphia. Because this platform was so spacious, high (24′ at the rear) and coarse, and because the openings and exposed timber supports of the house looked less substantial, the impression from below was that of a modern chalet placed lightly on the remains of a medieval fortress. Because the platform on which it rested looked as if it had been part of the hill for years, Chandler was able to raise the house and provide commanding views without suggesting that the building was detached from the site. The style of the house is difficult to determine precisely. The walls recalled the rough stonework of nineteenth-century English country houses, the gables and porches the Queen Anne style, and the woodwork the stick style (a modern designation) of the 1870s. This eclecticism inspired a writer for *Lippincott's Magazine,* which featured "Stonecliffe" in an article in April, 1884, to observe that now "there exist no fixed laws in modern architecture, and that we may expect almost every modification of form which sentiment, circumstances, and individual taste may suggest when offered entire free play." Far from the best example of "entire free play," this design was the most playful of the four by Chandler (plates 35, 38, 40) in this series. It was constructed of Chestnut Hill stone with dormers, balconies, and gables in white pine and roof of red slate. The bamboo blinds that shaded the great porches were unusual

in Chandler's work. The floors of the interior were of Georgia pine and three of the main floor rooms, the dining room (18′ × 25′), the morning room (20′ × 16′) and the parlor, were also finished in pine. However, the hall (22′ × 27′) was done in oak with a paneled and beamed ceiling, and the library (16′ × 18′) was paneled to the ceiling in ash. There were five bedrooms on the second floor and six bedrooms on the third. Located on Sunset Avenue off Norwood Avenue, the house no longer stands.

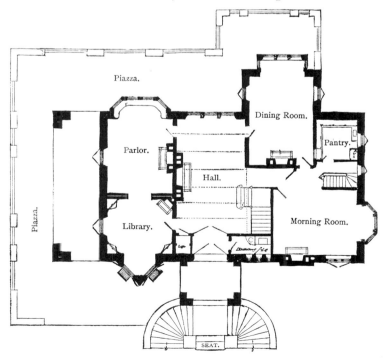

38. "Restrevor," Samuel B. Brown residence, Haverford, Pa.;
Theophilus P. Chandler, Jr., architect, 1881–84. The period in
which *Artistic Country-Seats* appeared is fascinating today for the
apparent inconsistencies that one often senses in the lives of those
who owned these houses and in the houses themselves. A progressive businessman, Brown (1843–1932) was credited by his
peers with hiring the first stenographer in Philadelphia, yet socially he did not risk looking foolish. He was a member of the
Union League Club and the Merion Cricket Club. Cricket was
the most popular sport among Philadelphia's elite at the end of
the century, and matches at the posh clubs—Germantown, Merion, Belmont—drew hundreds of the city's social leaders. Brown's
attraction to cricket complements the "Old World" flavor of this
house and the name he gave it, "Restrevor." Built with untrimmed
Haverford stone, the walls of the house acquired a patina of age
at birth, and this suggestion of age was reinforced by the high
roofs with outdated terra-cotta crestings, stepped or corbie gables
popular in northern Europe from the fourteenth through the seventeenth centuries, and the crenelation and tower of even earlier
periods. Chandler respected the grand tradition of architecture by
restating many of its tested forms and artistic devices; other architects respected the grand tradition by deemphasizing ornament
in favor of spatial and somatic issues. Fortunately, Sheldon, by
illustrating the work of both, documented differences of opinion
that were fundamental to the decade's architectural vitality. Chandler and Brown were not troubled by the brightly striped awnings
that festooned this venerable cliff nor the anachronistic stylistic
references outside and the electric bells, speaking tubes and telephones within because they enjoyed a freedom of expression
many architects and critics of the twentieth century have tried to

reprimand. Moreover, despite the expected compartmentalized
interior, the arrangement and treatment of rooms permitted views
from the dining room to the side piazza and from entrance door
to the stained-glass window of the landing. The ceiling and wainscoting of the hall (28′ × 18′) were of dark oak. An elaborately
carved fireplace was located diagonally opposite the stairway, and
between it and the main door was a curved lounge with an archway
separating it from the rest of the hall. The dining room (21′ × 17′)
was finished in cherry. From it, two archways led into the base
of the 64 -high tower and the conservatory. To the west were the
library (17′ × 28′) and the reception room, the former finished in
light oak with a mantel of the same wood and a facing of Wyoming
blue sandstone, and the latter carried out in maple. "Restrevor,"
built at the corner of Rose Lane and Booth Lane, no longer stands.

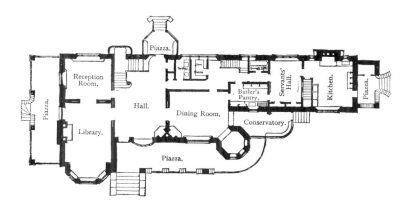

39. "Kragsyde," George Nixon Black residence, Manchester-by-the-Sea, Mass.; Peabody and Stearns, architects, 1884. This house was set in the wooded, craggy heights overlooking the Atlantic north of Boston. In 1882 the Blacks purchased six acres of land at picturesque Manchester and hired fellow Bostonians to design their summer house and stables—riding and driving were popular pastimes—and famed landscape architect Frederick Law Olmsted to lay out the grounds. One's first impression of eccentric disorder is quickly restrained by an appreciation of the chaotic but spirited unity that ultimately triumphs. Critics then and now have praised its unusual, beguiling appearance. Vincent Scully contended that despite their free thinking, Peabody and Stearns never again "created a house of such quality." Unwittingly, they produced a remarkable, photogenic building at a time when architects were unaware of the powerful influence photography was to exert on architectural design. The tactile surfaces of natural shingles and roughly laid local stone, the plastic activity of projections and voids, the struggle between expanding volumes and the fragile wooden envelope—all register as stimulating effects in a two-dimensional picture. Furthermore, the compositional movements of "Kragsyde" were so strong that the photograph suggests a candid shot of a mobile object. Because of its size, shape and asymmetry, the Black house could not be understood from a single point. While a photograph of it could only do justice to one of its faces, it could also whet the viewer's desire to know what existed beyond the visible fragment. In this case the photographer concentrated on the entrance wing (20′ × 55′), emphasizing its dark, protective voids rather than the more outgoing main section (75′ × 45′). If a photograph can shape a building's statement, it can also single out particular functions. Here the shot downplays the frequent acts of sitting, talking, reading, watching—those daily private or social activities that occurred on piazzas attached to each of the main rooms—and, instead, reminds us of the impact of departures and arrivals on the cadence of summer life. We even see the small window within the arch behind which family sentinels could sit to watch for relatives and friends. The entranceway of 11 steps was dark. From darkness one walked up five more steps into light and toward the magnificent vistas offered by the hall with its comfortable, built-in seats and its attached piazza. At the rear right of the hall were steps that led to the angled corridor and the boudoir-library over the arch. Black, who died in 1928, leaving an estate of $5 million, was a major benefactor of Boston's cultural and medical agencies. The house, which cost approximately $60,000, was destroyed in 1929.

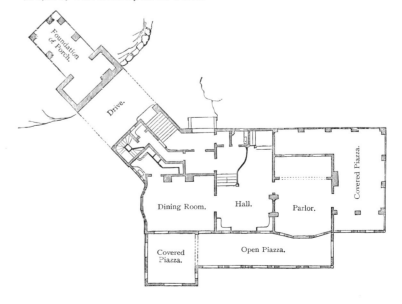

40. Edwin N. Benson residence, Philadelphia, Pa.; Theophilus P. Chandler, Jr., architect, 1884. In an article about Chestnut Hill in *Lippincott's Magazine* of April, 1884, the author illustrated the ruins of Benson's first house on this site and wrote about the lonely silhouette of its charred remains. Judging from this photograph of the second house, Benson must have vowed that never again would fire, or for that matter, storm, earthquake, pestilence or sword destroy his castle. Built in the year that the article appeared, it remained the largest and the costliest residence of this elegant suburb during the 1880s. To protect it from another conflagration, Benson insisted on interior partitions of brick, plastering on wire instead of wood lathe, asbestos paper between the floors, mortar finish for all air spaces, and a special staircase on the north side which from top to bottom was made of slate with brick walls. Despite his efforts, the house has been demolished. S. F. Hotchkin, writing about Chestnut Hill in 1889, observed that, standing before the house, it was easy "to imagine yourself in 'merrie England.' . . . So English is the scene that one almost looks to see the sentinel standing by the massive stone gate posts." English fever swept these Philadelphia suburbs in the 1880s. It was manifested not only in the architecture of many of the residences built during the decade but also in the regional enthusiasm for cricket or for hare and hounds, a bloodless variation of the British original in which colorfully garbed men and women played cops and robbers on horseback. In this house Chandler once again chose local stone for the exterior. It was gray while the tile roof was soft red. Sheldon asserted that Chandler used stone because he believed a nation could not have an architectural history without building in stone. There were many people in the United States who shared this opinion and an even greater number in Europe, where most designers and critics considered a respectable wooden house a contradiction in terms. Sheldon also contended that the architect had listened carefully to the advice of landscape architect A. J. Downing, who once declared, "We believe that artists and men of taste have agreed that all forms of acknowledged beauty are composed of curved lines." Chandler may have been unaware of such arguments, but he certainly attempted to modify the hardness of the

right angle by frequently inserting curved forms. The dimensions of the house were exceptionally large; the piazza was at least 120' long and the length from parlor wall to dining-room wall was 92'. The rooms must have been impressive in finish as well as in scale. The hall (50' × 24') had an elaborate oak ceiling, paneled staircase of oak and stained-glass windows. The dining room (30' long) was finished in chestnut, the 20'-square parlor was done in butternut and the billiard room (19' × 24') in quartered oak. The house stood on the south side of Bethlehem Pike, east of Stenton Avenue.

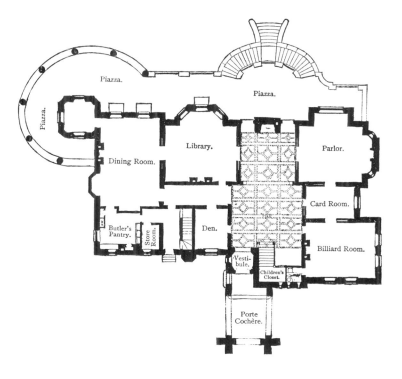

41. James Hopkins Smith residence, Falmouth Foreside, Me.; John Calvin Stevens, architect, 1885. "One rarely sees so much breadth, so much roominess, and so much solidity obtained with so small an outlay of money [$7,000]. Effect has been sought by strength of mass and simplicity of form." Sheldon's enthusiasm for this house, so simple yet so summary of the architectural thought of the mid-1880s, was justified. Stevens created a rock base that implies being of, as well as on, the ground. Taken from a farm wall, the stones were laid with their surfaces of gray mosses and lichens exposed. On top of this base he placed a light, trim and controlled container that makes us aware of the internal volumes we ignored when admiring the rugged walls below. Through contrasts he achieved an unusual, persistently threatened unity: the contrast of weighty stone and light, brown-stained shingles, of protection below and goodwill above, of immobility and graceful lines, of randomness and forethought. Stevens used the stalwart circular wall and stone arch to stage the void beyond them. He avoided the appearance of rigidity in the shingled planes by means of the prominent dormers and the asymmetrically placed windows, and by gently breaking their flatness above the large bay of windows and below the windows between the dormers. Although the Smith house resembles closely the gambrel-roof structures of the Colonial period, Stevens' brilliant response to contemporary and particular requirements transcends the plagiarism of old form. The plan is simple and efficient. Because the piazza, in effect, was treated as a vestibule, the stone fireplaces of both hall and parlor immediately stood out, though their roles in the plan differed. The former was a central mass around which space leaked, while the latter was presented as the conclusion of a spatial experience. By placing the hall and parlor on the same axis and connecting both to the piazza by high French doors, the architect stressed their functional relatedness and their relative dissimilarity to the isolated, formal dining room. The ceiling of the dining room was finished in panels of bamboo while the other rooms were finished in natural or painted pine. The rear of the house, located at 143 Foreside Road, has been extensively altered. Stevens (1855–1940) used his skill with pencil, pen and brush to celebrate architecture as a painterly rather than a linear art. Though he designed many nonresidential structures in Maine, he is best known today for his domestic work. His partnership with Albert Cobb (1868–1941) began in 1885 or 1886 and lasted until 1891. In 1889 the two published an important study of the period, *Examples of American Domestic Architecture*, in which Cobb was responsible for the text and Stevens for the illustrations. J. H. Smith (1847–1932) traced his line to the brother of Captain John Smith. After early successes in the sugar industry and railroads, he retired at the age of 30, dividing his time between New York City and Falmouth.

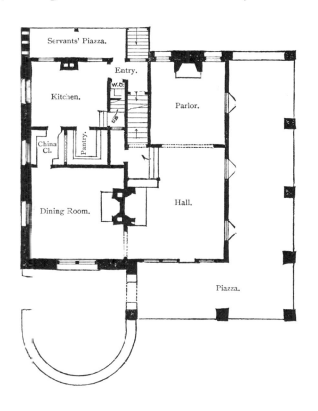

42. "Ballytore," Isaac H. Clothier residence, Wynnewood, Pa.; Addison Hutton, architect, 1885. Hutton (1834–1916) came to Philadelphia in 1857. Trained by his father as a carpenter, he became an apprentice in the office of Samuel Sloan and in 1863 opened his own practice. A year later he joined Sloan in partnership, an arrangement that lasted until 1868. He remained a significant architect of Philadelphia for the next three decades, designing churches, business buildings, campus architecture for Bryn Mawr, Haverford and Lehigh, and many suburban houses. George Tatum observed that "Hutton was among the last of his generation who would continue to receive major commissions despite the fact that he had never had the advantage of instruction at the French École or at one of the American schools patterned after it." Clothier, born in 1837, was a dry-goods merchant who joined another Quaker, Justus C. Strawbridge, to form in 1862 Strawbridge & Clothier, one of the notable department stores of the city. He retired from business in 1895. Many of the features that distinguish the Philadelphia houses included in this series are evident here. The site is rolling, attractive and spacious (50 acres), the dimensions of the foundation generous (120' × at least 40'), the skyline noticeable (the tower is 80' high) and irregular, the style mixed and the impression dignified but not dull. Furthermore, visual interest is developed from the combination of forms and masses rather than through applied ornament, and the color scheme of gray granite, Wyoming Valley bluestone for bands and copings, and the blue slate roof is restrained. The eclectic design of "Ballytore" looked old-fashioned beside the work of younger and more experimental designers of the 1880s, but its plan was more representative. Hutton arranged the socially important rooms along an axis facing the pleasant landscape toward the southeast and, reserving the front of the house for traffic and reception, effectively isolated the study. Wide openings link several rooms, and the break between the library and parlor dou-

bles as a pathway to the rear porch. Hutton showed more courage than many by placing the elevator in a relatively prominent location. Sheldon's comments about the Clothier house are very revealing. He praised Hutton for adapting construction to meet modern needs; "a mere glance at the structural lines of this house shows how simple and useful they are." He liked the choice of material, stating, in effect, that everyone agreed that stone was a better material for houses than wood. He lauded the architect for choosing free composition over academic conventions. These assertions, somewhat debatable, nevertheless tell us that Sheldon was comfortable with this kind of house, probably more comfortable than he was with the pacesetting shingle houses, which caught his fancy but failed to convince his good judgment. For many years known as the Agnes Irwin School and located at the corner of Lancaster Pike and Wynnewood Avenue, "Ballytore" has been converted into an Armenian church.

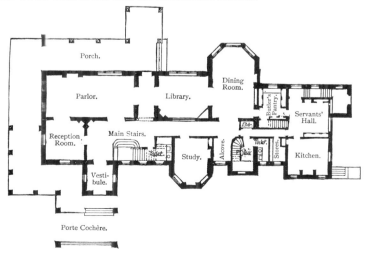

43. P. E. Van Riper residence, Montclair, N.J.; Francis H. Kimball, architect, 1884–86. This sturdy, modestly pretentious suburban house, built at the corner of Fullerton Avenue and Union Street, no longer exists. Although Kimball (1845–1919) was not an outstanding designer of domestic spaces and exterior effects, he nevertheless pleased clients who wanted substantial-looking homes with contemporary features and conveniences and a touch of class. His plan for the Van Riper house was sensibly conceived: a square hall, static in movement and centrally located, led to the principal rooms as well as the kitchen area. His execution, however, was not subtle. Didactically, he included three distinct areas—porch, vestibule and forehall—prior to the hall. In contradistinction to the hall, he created a circular-ended parlor which was centrifugal in movement and brightly lighted. Similar contrasts existed between the hall and library, but he changed the shape of the library's projection to avoid duplicating the perimeter of the parlor. Affirming that dining was the most formal of all social activities, he chose simple geometry over fanciful shapes. His implementation of a workable plan was, thus, somewhat self-conscious. Designing in a period of rapid technological change and expansion, the task of architects became more complicated. Functional obligations threatened artistic visions. For example, Kimball had to incorporate furnace units that supplied steam heat to the first floor and hot air to the second. A gas pump in the basement lifted water to a tank in the attic which, in turn, replenished toilet tanks on lower floors. He also had to contend with social conventions. The forehall was an acceptable location for a gentleman's lavatory but not for a lady's. Areas of the house, formerly simple, now challenged the architect's skill. The attic in the Van Riper house contained, in addition to the tank room, the stairwell, two servants' rooms, a storage space and a 24′ square billiard parlor. Although Kimball probably subscribed to the view that interior use shaped exterior expression, he interpreted this relationship of cause and effect freely as the respective impacts on the exterior of the circular wall of the parlor and octagonal projection of the library indicate. Information about the owner is scarce. Peter E. Van Riper worked for the North River Blue Stone Co. in New York City in 1890 and later in the decade was a broker with offices at 60 Broadway. Kimball practiced in New York, where, with Thomas Wisedell, he designed the exotic Casino Theatre in 1882 and, with George Thompson, the Manhattan Life Insurance Co. skyscraper in the early 1890s.

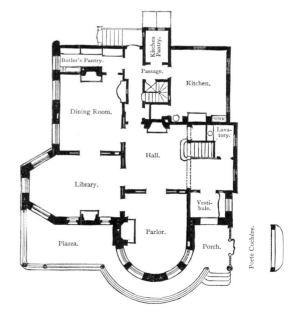

44. Addison G. Foster residence, St. Paul, Minn.; Clarence H. Johnston, architect, 1883. Although Sheldon found examples of country seats in the pleasant suburbs of such Eastern cities as Boston and Philadelphia, those he included from Minnesota were located within the city limits of Minneapolis and St. Paul. Was he, an Easterner, implying that the cities of the "Northwest" were somewhat rural in flavor? The four houses he selected from St. Paul were all located on Summit Avenue, a street of large and often ostentatious residences that remains today one of the finest urban records of late nineteenth-century taste and aspirations. However, the range of critical response to this architecture of Summit Avenue has been wide, from Frank Lloyd Wright's condemnation—"the worst collection of architecture in the entire world"—to contemporaneous praise—"liberal expenditure without ostentation, directed by skill and restrained by taste." Foster (b. 1837) came to Minnesota from Massachusetts in 1859, entered the lumber business three years later and, in the late 1880s, moved to Tacoma, Wash. to become vice-president of the St. Paul and Tacoma Lumber Co. He represented the state of Washington in the United States Senate from 1899 to 1905. Unlike the majority of lumber barons of the day, Foster commissioned a house built of pressed red brick; undoubtedly, its prestigious location affected his decision. Still standing at 490 Summit Avenue, his $35,000 residence measures 50′ wide and 72′ deep. Instead of designing an exterior in which the sections were clearly subordinated to the whole, Johnston highlighted three distinct parts: the porches, marked by the quick movements of the stickwork; the solid, quiet surfaces of the lower floors; and the roof with its intentional stylistic contradictions. Despite the severe winter temperatures in the area, or because of the warm summers, the ceilings are high: basement 8′, first story 11′, second story 10½′, and the attic, where the billiard room was located, 9′. The plan of this house and that of the Griggs house (plate 46), also by Johnston, share several common features. Both are elongated with the short side facing the street. Through the center runs a narrow, segmented hall that is met deep within the plan by a side hall. Johnston was unable to incorporate stairways gracefully into these plans. His preference for toilet rooms and large cloak closets on the first floor had not yet become common. On the other hand, he may have been criticized for placing the toilet of the Foster house too close to the dining room, for some, in the politest of companies, argued that the sound of flushed human waste was inimicable to the desired atmosphere of a formal dinner. Clarence Johnston (1859–1936) settled in St. Paul after studying at the Massachusetts Institute of Technology. Though a rather dry designer, he was eulogized in obituaries for his service to both his profession and the state of Minnesota. He designed many of the buildings of the new campus of the University of Minnesota.

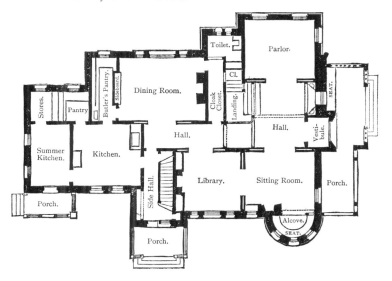

45. Potter Palmer residence, Chicago, Ill.; Cobb and Frost, architects, 1885. After Palmer arrived in Chicago in 1852, he became an experimental dry-goods merchant, built the famous Palmer House hotel (which he rebuilt after the fire of 1871) and speculated successfully in real estate. Though Potter built this castellated Gothic structure, his wife, Bertha Honoré Palmer, set its tone. She was a memorable woman who died in 1918, 16 years after her husband. An intelligent doll who wore his lavish gifts, she was also a strong individual who fought vigorously for a female presence at the Columbian Exposition of 1893 and for the acceptance of such unconventional artists as Monet, Corot and Pissarro. The house, 80′ × 56′, constructed of Connecticut brownstone and Amherst stone from Ohio, stood at Lake Shore Drive and Banks Street until it was demolished in 1951. Its exterior was finished in 1883 and the interior work, entrusted to the Chicago firm of Silsbee and Kent, was begun in January 1884. The striped surface, influenced by English Victorian polychromy, dazzled the eye as effectively as it frustrated systematic attempts to understand supporting form. The large rooms, such as the dining room (24′ × 32′), decorated by the famed Herter Brothers firm of New York, and the drawing room (22′ × 42′), opened widely to the hall, enabling guests to circulate easily. David Lowe made an excellent point in *Chicago Interiors:* the "castle, with its exteriors designed by one set of architects, its interiors by another, and its decoration in the hands of still other men, is a kind of symbol." It was a symbol of architecture that consciously rejected the vaunted unity of art in favor of an eclecticism of objects and styles. If we are inclined to repudiate it as collage architecture, we must first remember that its owners considered it a demonstration of the power of art as a transforming force of society. The Palmers took art seriously and were willing to pay to make this point clear. The nursery, for example, was finished in Hungarian ash, ebony and white holly, with wainscoting four feet high. If the Palmers' support of art was generous, it was also liberal. Unlike some in the nineteenth century who agonized over the threat of science to art,

the Palmers' open-mindedness embraced technology. Mrs. Palmer's Moorish bedroom, reached by one of the first domestic elevators in Chicago, had its walls painted after Turkish designs, its windows similar to those in the Palace in Cairo and its woodwork ebony and gold. The principal architects for the house were Henry Ives Cobb (1859–1931) and Charles S. Frost (1856–1932). Cobb moved from the office of Peabody and Stearns to Chicago in the early 1880s. Among his best-known Romanesque Revival designs were the Newberry Library (1887) and the Fisheries Building for the Columbian Exposition of 1893. In 1902 he relocated his office in New York City.

46. Chauncey W. Griggs residence, St. Paul, Minn.; Clarence H. Johnston, architect, 1883. Some similarities between this plan and the plan of the Foster house (plate 44) have already been noted. Additionally, the major rooms of the first floors of both houses were square or rectangular except those rooms—the sitting room of the Foster house and Mr. Griggs's room (the library)—that were meant to be less formal. In both plans Johnston paired a family room and a social room at the front and placed the dining room toward the rear. Each dining room, adjacent to the kitchen and reached through the butler's pantry, contained a substantial fireplace, adequate natural lighting and a built-in sideboard. In each, the sideboard was located as close as possible to the entrance from the butler's pantry, a decision that informs us about the architect's priorities and the struggle between convenience and convention in the 1880s. Obviously, Johnston was concerned about serving the food hot, restricting the steps of those serving and making the servants less conspicuous. By eliminating windows above or at the ends of the sideboards, he attempted to prevent the food from looking washed out. He also questioned current conventions that held that the sideboard should have a wall all to itself and that it be placed at the end of the room behind the chair of the mistress or master of the house. The rooms of the main floor were finished in hardwood—cherry for the library and dining room and bird's-eye maple for the reception room and music room. The tone of the interior was set by the hall. Wainscoted and beamed with oak, its course was interrupted by thick, molded arches and by the grand stairway with its full landing, triple window and domed, paneled ceiling. Exclusive of halls and service spaces, there were 22 rooms in this $50,000 house. New domestic, labor-saving devices, such as the elevator, radiating steam heat and electrical wiring, all of which were installed in the Griggs house, appeared in the major cities before they were tried in the country. This modern Romanesque structure was built of Lake Superior sand-stone. The gables of Akron tiles and roof of slate are not well integrated with the stone base; this is most evident where the tower breaks through the roof. Measuring 90′ × 55′ on an original lot of 100′ × 190′, the house still stands at 476 Summit Avenue. Griggs was born in Tolland, Conn. in 1832 and died in Tacoma, Wash. in 1910. Settling in St. Paul in 1856, he became merchant, grocer, railroad builder, coal dealer, lumberman, banker and served in the Minnesota legislature. In the late 1880s he moved to Tacoma, Wash. to head the St. Paul and Tacoma Lumber Co.

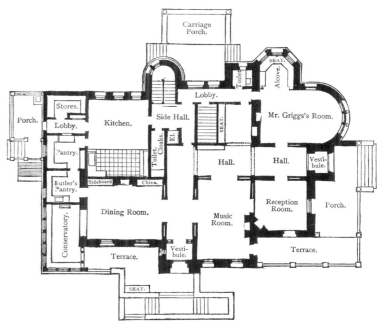

47. Sylvester T. Everett residence, Cleveland, O.; Charles F. Schweinfurth, architect, 1883. When this house was completed on Euclid Avenue after three years of construction, it was the finest and costliest mansion on that elegant thoroughfare. Its dimensions (70′ × 120′) accounted for much of the final bill of $225,000, as did the brownstone brought from Hummelstown, Pa., but Everett, who could afford it, was also willing to pay for the safest and healthiest construction and for handcrafted decoration. Built with iron beams, with an iron roof, fire-resistant blocks for minor partitions and brick walls for main partitions, it was probably one of the best fireproofed houses of the day. Special vents in the kitchen introduced fresh air and removed stale air. Each of the ten bedrooms had a fireplace, a book alcove, a dressing room and a bathroom, and each was finished in its own particular hardwood. All of the stained glass of the interior was designed by Louis Comfort Tiffany, and the heads on the exterior were taken from models made by the architect. Despite all of the cost and effort, the house lasted only 55 years. Its Richardsonian Romanesque design, suggesting simplicity without monotony, strength that was not static, stability that could tolerate the moderate excitement of the attic floor and, in general, rugged self-reliance, evidently projected the image Everett wanted. He was a formidable figure of Cleveland's post-Civil War boom, one who was successful regardless of the enterprise—banking, steel, railroads, mining, ranching. Among the distinguished visitors to the house were Andrew Carnegie and J. P. Morgan and, because Everett was a strong Republican, Presidents Grant, Hayes, McKinley and Taft. The main floor plan was simple but effective. The hall must have made a dramatic impression upon guests who entered from the heavy porte-cochere and the somewhat constricted vestibule. Immediately, they must have sensed they were in a significant space—broad (24′), long (54′), uncluttered and anchored at the opposite end by a massive fireplace. This room was paneled in

oak and richly decorated with Romanesque carving, while above, the domed ceiling was supported by ribs of the same wood. The conversation piece of the interior was undoubtedly the small semicircular balcony on which Mrs. Everett stood to greet couples as they climbed the stairs to the third-floor ballroom. With its Moorish effects, sandalwood paneling and carved wishing well, the ballroom probably merited a special introduction. Everett was responsible for bringing Schweinfurth (1856–1919), who previously had worked in the East, to Cleveland, where his major role in the late nineteenth-century architecture of that city is undisputed today. With 15 mansions to his credit, Schweinfurth, according to Eric Johannesen, was "the premier residential architect of Euclid Avenue."

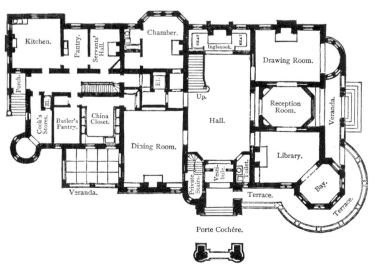

48. Frederick Driscoll residence, St. Paul, Minn.; William H. Willcox, architect, 1884. In this flamboyant period, the size, spatial complexity and finish of the houses Sheldon selected reveal the vitality of their designers and the bank accounts of their owners. Created without hesitation or apology and financed by large sums, their artistic merit, on the other hand, was noticeably uneven, as was the artistic merit of American architecture in general. Ostensibly these photographs were included because they illustrated the latest and the finest American domestic work, yet the Driscoll house lacked the unity and even the contemporaneity of most of the houses by Emerson, Price or Little. There is no clear explanation for its inclusion. Perhaps Sheldon's criteria were extremely flexible. Perhaps the photographs were selected by a committee. Perhaps the subscribers influenced the selection of houses. Unquestionably, Sheldon was generous, referring to the Driscoll house as a unified version of the modern English style and claiming that its architect planned it "not only with a due regard to local consideration, but with an intelligent appreciation of the relations of architecture to construction." As he was often prone to do, Sheldon made authoritative-sounding generalizations which he did not explain. For example, he did not offer evidence to clarify how the elevation showed the unity of the modern English style nor how the architecture and the construction of this house had been intelligently integrated. Built of Lake Superior sandstone and Chicago pressed brick, it is extant at 266 Summit Avenue but, according to *A Guide to the Architecture of Minnesota* by Gebhard and Martinson, it is known today as Epiphany House. From the octagonal tower at the rear, the family had a magnificent view of the Mississippi below and could follow the course of the river for several miles in both directions. Despite sliding doors that imply that adjacent rooms can be joined into one larger room, Willcox conceived of his major spaces as separate functional areas. These are clustered around a large section that calls attention to the importance of entering and climbing. In the parlor and dining room the fireplace alcoves and built-in sideboard are sculpturally

rather than spatially conceived. The mahogany of the parlor and cherry of the living room were common woods for an imposing city house, but the red and white oak of the dining room was an unusual combination. It was also common to finish the second-floor rooms in a cheaper material such as the Georgia pine that was used. The lesser-known partner of Willcox and Johnston, Willcox apparently left St. Paul for Tacoma, Wash. in the 1890s. Driscoll was born in Boston in 1834 and was business manager of the *Pioneer Press* in St. Paul in the 1880s.

49. Mary Hemenway residence, Manchester-by-the-Sea, Mass.; William R. Emerson, architect, 1884. William Ralph Emerson (1833–1917) was a distant relative of Ralph Waldo Emerson. He moved from Illinois to Boston where, in the 1850s, he opened his office. As a founding member of the Boston Society of Architects in 1867, he contributed to the widespread movement to standardize the architectural profession, but his lofty place among domestic architects of the late nineteenth century is due primarily to his distinctive plans and, particularly, his elevations. Few designers had more faith in the expressive possibilities of the ordinary shingle, and few were able to compete with Emerson in creating such skillful and visually delightful variations with this basic unit. In rocky, timbered places like Manchester-by-the-Sea and Bar Harbor, he seemed most at home in the early 1880s. Mariana van Rensselaer wrote in the *Century Magazine* in 1886 that this house "seems almost as much a part of nature's first intentions as do the rocks and trees themselves." Uncut fieldstone from the property was used for the walls of the first floor. Emerson sank the house into the hillside by blasting out the basement. The primitive appearance of this kind of foundation, which impressed several European observers as an appropriately rugged statement for a young and untamed land, differed noticeably from the shingles. The surfaces of the upper floors suggested controlled energy and movement. Avoiding stylistic clichés, Emerson decorated this house with patterns: the wavy layers of shingles at the top of the gable and the scalloped ones below, the fragile latticework of the balcony, the methodical rhythm of the corner voids, the reiteration of the dormers to the right. His country-house plans were usually arranged to provide good views of the surroundings and were open to permit diagonal internal vistas. The former is true of the Hemenway house, but the plan is rigid. The two family rooms, the parlor and the dining room, are symmetrical, self-contained shapes. The hall becomes a narrow, relatively dark corridor for traffic. Access to the stairway through the parlor is unusual. This floor is finished in hardwoods, the second and third in pine. Built for approximately $15,000, this house is still standing but has been altered, according to the foremost authority on Emerson, Cynthia Zaitzevsky. The Hemenway house was built for the widow of Augustus Hemenway (1805–1876), who had made a fortune trading with the west coast of South America and with China. Mary Hemenway, who died in 1894, used her wealth to support orphanages, Indian schools and educational institutions in Boston.

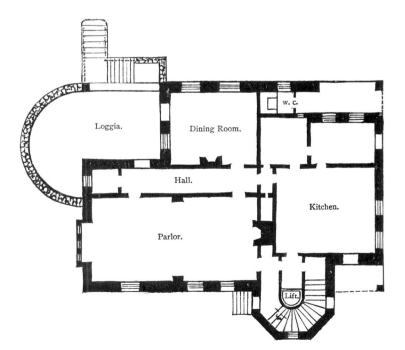

50. Henry R. Mallory residence, Bryam, Conn.; Lamb and Rich, architects, ca. 1885. Mallory (1848–1919) represented the eighth generation of his family in America and the fourth to be active in shipping. In his father's firm, H. C. Mallory & Co., he rose rapidly from ordinary office boy at the age of 18 to partner at 20 and, eventually, to president. In later years he spent more time at Bryam than he did at his Brooklyn residence. Sheldon explained that he included this house not because it was costly, large or unusual but because it was "an example of a pure spirit in architecture." By this he meant that it answered its requirements directly, pleasantly and economically. Unable to name the style in which it was designed—Vincent Scully christened it the "Shingle Style" in the 1950s—he, nevertheless, thought it looked like an appropriate American expression, certainly better than the Queen Anne style, which he referred to as a "craze." Shingles covered the prominent gables and the second floor, and clapboards the lower floor. However, this style was characterized by more than its material; it often expressed the freedom, confidence, imagination and energy of its numerous designers, traits revealed directly by the Mallory exterior. This was the kind of American house that caught the eye of Jean Boussard and several other French critics in the mid-1880s. Convinced that conventions and formalism were stultifying French architecture, they directed the attention of their readers to this kind of house, calling it "refreshing" and "curiously instructive." To them the veranda of the Mallory house would have been a useful space but, more important, because they were decrying the sterility of contemporary French architecture, also the source of mysterious voids that contrasted starkly with the tactile supports. The dramatic gable, conceivably indiscreet, would, nevertheless, have been evidence of artistic vigor. The eclectic ornament, a sign of poor training to some in Paris, would have been proof of the Americans' escape from the tyranny of the grand tradition. However, the French of the 1880s did not see and appreciate what we dote on today. They would have admired the artistic verve of this elevation; we laud its spatial aggressiveness, the push-pull tug of its masses and the flux of its rippling surfaces. Similarly, had they seen its interior, they would have envied the designers' disregard of the "empty rules of symmetry" or praised the "bizarre" and "unskilled" yet "sincere and expressive" decoration. They would not have shared our present-day enthusiasm for space as an active agent, for its casual, unencumbered flow between hall and parlor. This house, off Bryam Road, is still standing.

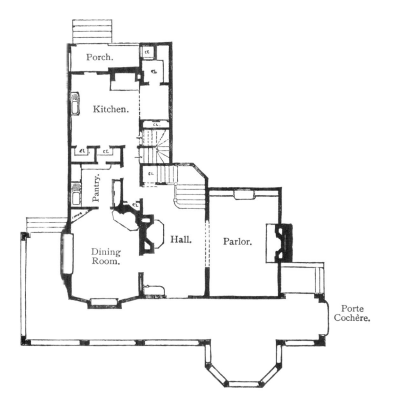

51. "Mossley Hall," William B. Howard residence, Mount Desert, Me.; William R. Emerson, architect, 1883. Thanks to Cynthia Zaitzevsky's research, we know that in April, 1883 the Mount Desert *Herald* called the almost-finished Howard house "the largest private residence . . . on the island." Approximately 125' from one wing tip to the other, this "summer cottage," bearing the heavy name of "Mossley Hall," meandered across the hill, acquiring in the process a plethora of views of both water and mountains. To an age gradually realizing that resources are not limitless, such a house, used for only a fraction of the year by one family, may seem even more exotic than it did to those who saw it in the 1880s. At that time men of means such as Howard could purchase vast and unsullied parcels of ground and erect private wooden castles the size of small hotels without justifying the efficiency of the space or the frequency of use. The dimensions of the major rooms were not petty: the hall 38' × 22', library 17' × 22', parlor 21' × 31', dining room 24' × 25' and billiard room of the tower 17' × 25'. When the sliding doors between the hall and parlor were opened, the space between the fireplace and the wide bay window was almost 50 feet. The grandeur of these spaces and the fine woods in which they were finished—cherry for the dining room and stained antique oak for the hall—remind us that, while life in these country seats was more relaxed and informal than life in the city house, a proper social atmosphere was still maintained. Emerson included a lookout by the hall fireplace from which visitors could admire the spectacular scenery and, on a lower level, a musicians' gallery. However, it was the exterior that revealed his ingenuity and imagination most effectively. Once again he took the site seriously, sustaining and even enhancing its magic. Vincent Scully referred to it as "a nineteenth-century landscape painter's ideal of an upland dwelling." The strength of the foreground rocks was acknowledged in the stone foundation, but the dominant impression of the elevation was movement. This movement was generated, in part, by the irregular skyline composed of variations on the conifer form. On the sides the light dances over the independent planes of stained shingles. These planes coalesced tenuously, their precise location in space difficult to determine. Consequently the house impresses us as a visual illusion rather than a material fact. Emerson has demonstrated brilliantly the painterly potential of architecture. "Mossley Hall," built for approximately $50,000, was one of 70 houses destroyed in the fire that swept Mount Desert in 1947. William B. Howard (1833–1898) of New York and Chicago, head of one of the largest construction firms in the country, built the Nickel Plate Railroad.

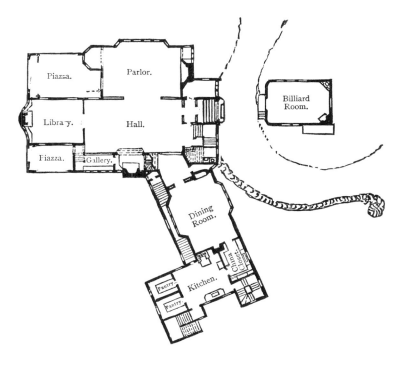

52. Narragansett Pier Casino, Narragansett Pier, R.I.; McKim, Mead & White, architects, 1886. This resort first attracted summer visitors in 1845 and a few years later some cottages were built but, unlike the social structure of Newport across the bay, the cottage contingent remained relatively small. The Narragansett crowd was distinctively young, boisterous, athletic, flirtatious and not greatly concerned about dress or proper etiquette. "Perhaps at no other watering place in the world does one so often encounter the startling sight of a gentleman in bathing suit conversing calmly with a lady in elaborate toilet." In 1883 a corporation was formed to find a suitable site and hire an architect. McKim evidently was in charge of the project and, with the assistance of White, designed the building that year. Completed in the summer of 1886 at a cost of $66,480, the Casino was the focal point for some 5,000 daily visitors during the height of the season in August. The routine varied little. In the late morning vacationers went to the Casino to read mail, write letters, watch tennis matches and move from one conversational cluster to another. Bathing time lasted from noon until one o'clock when the bathers dressed for the "morning" concert followed by dinner, then more exercise—walking, driving, tennis—until supper time. The evenings were reserved for parties, dinners, concerts and, twice a week, hops. The great stone archway still spans Ocean Avenue, but the framed parts of the original building have been destroyed by fires and storms. The whole complex, poorly revealed in the photograph, was an odd marriage between the robust arch and its tower buttresses and the meandering and relatively fragile wooden extension. The peculiarity of this combination can be partially understood by examining the portion that remains. The mood of the stone base is heavy, serious, protective, even threatening. Above, the design is playful to the extent that it is intentionally undisciplined. Look closely at the uneven surface of the roof between the dormers and the irregular layers of shingles. Leland Roth claims that McKim once climbed

the roof and twisted some shingles to express such whimsy more dramatically. The ground floor was entered through the ominous cavity under the arch. The steps led to a hallway through which one reached the piazza. Along the piazza were the doorways to the private dining rooms and main dining room, 34' × 57', the only space with porches on both sides. The principal piazza was duplicated on the second floor. A billiard room was also available on this level while the main space of the enclosed third floor was a rather plain theater. The most popular congregating spot was unquestionably the open stone porch over the arch.

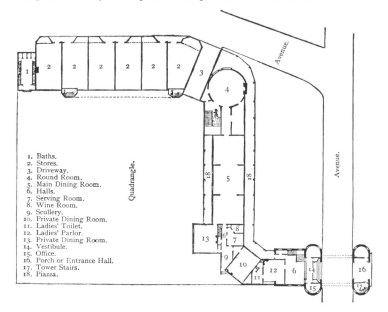

1. Baths.
2. Stores.
3. Driveway.
4. Round Room.
5. Main Dining Room.
6. Halls.
7. Serving Room.
8. Wine Room.
9. Scullery.
10. Private Dining Room.
11. Ladies' Toilet.
12. Ladies' Parlor.
13. Private Dining Room.
14. Vestibule.
15. Office.
16. Porch or Entrance Hall.
17. Tower Stairs.
18. Piazza.

53. Henry A. C. Taylor residence, Newport, R.I.; McKim, Mead & White, architects, 1886. The Taylor house on Annandale Road, demolished in 1952, has been discussed numerous times by critics and historians since it was completed in 1886. Sheldon called its style "very nearly a pure colonial." Mariana van Rensselaer, in her three-part article on American houses in the *Century Magazine*, May–July, 1886, viewed the house as an attempt to adapt the colonial style to contemporary interior planning. In 1944 Henry-Russell Hitchcock saw it as the "decisive step" in the stages of the Colonial Revival, and 11 years later Vincent Scully, agreeing to its importance, contended that it "had two diverging effects upon later developments: one toward order *per se*, the other toward academicism and eclecticism." Recently, William B. Rhoads, while acknowledging that it was the "culmination of this turn toward order," also cautioned that its "amplitude and abundance of ornament" were Victorian rather than Colonial. In the 1880s observers tended to praise the Taylor house because it was a reassuring alternative to the exuberance of the Queen Anne style and the spatial intricacies of shingled houses. In recent decades, critics have acknowledged its eighteenth-century sources and McKim's careful organization but have tended to view its success as a large nail in the coffin of innovative design and planning. Wrote Scully, "The Taylor House and its descendants made antiquarianism respectable and originality suspect." The "antiquarian" elements were the lightly colored clapboard walls with white trim, the Palladian or Venetian windows (three lights, the middle wider, higher and often arched), the garlanding, balustrades, Ionic porches, symmetrical organization, landing window, etc. With its central hallway and balanced corner rooms, the plan also reflected eighteenth-century American interiors. Conversely, the number of Palladian windows and Ionic porches, the dwarfed entranceway overwhelmed by the landing window, the irregularly laid shingles (to suggest the time-worn sag of the roof) and the intimate rela-

tionship between house and the lawn on the ocean side were not characteristic of eighteenth-century work. On the other side, however, the sloping ground necessitated a higher base and a more formal relationship between the house and lawn. The house's dimensions were 138' × 62' and its cost between $65,800 and $75,000. The first sketches were done in 1882, in 1884 it was redesigned for wood rather than masonry, and construction began in 1885. It was commissioned by Henry A. Coit Taylor (d. 1921), son of Moses Taylor, who left 40 million dollars at his death in 1882. Classified as a New York financier, Henry was associated with several railroads, the National City Bank of New York, the New York Life Insurance and Trust Co. and the Newport Trust Co.

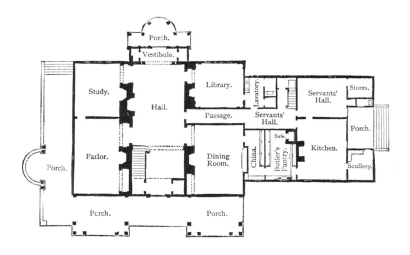

54. Harry L. Laws residence, Cincinnati, O.; James W. Mc-Laughlin, architect, ca. 1886. This house was built sometime between August, 1885 when the plans were dated and the publication of the Cincinnati Directory of 1886, the first to indicate that the Laws family was residing at 3003 Reading Road in Walnut Hills. Harry Laws was a prominent figure in the city's commercial, civic and social affairs. Born in Cincinnati in 1852 and educated in local schools, he began clerking at the age of 17. Four years later he joined his father's firm, James H. Laws & Co., commission merchants. In 1878 he began a profitable venture in the sugar trade of Louisiana and after the turn of the century served as a director of several of Cincinnati's banks. Laws became Hamilton County's ninety-sixth traffic fatality for 1923 when he was hit by a car on September 28. He was 33 when he asked James Mc-Laughlin, dean of Cincinnati's architects, to design this large, substantial residence. Its plan, more than its elevation, linked McLaughlin (b. 1834) with an older generation of American architects. Despite sliding doors, he conceived of spaces as formal and functionally distinct units to be experienced in measured sequence. Pedantically, the plan called attention to the beauty and integrity of each of the major rooms of the first floor. Granted, he varied these spaces through bays and nooks and initially confronted visitors with the gentle curves of the veranda, but his main objective was an interior divided neatly into proper, precious and virtually symmetrical sections. Although the elevation was somewhat more representative of this series than the plan, the hall was unusually wide for this type of interior. Sheldon praised the "extreme simplicity and solidity" of the Laws house; he viewed it as an alternative to the picturesque, vernacular appearance of other houses he included. Compared to McLaughlin's Netter house (plate 57) of 1881, this was more restrained and better unified. Although the architect incorporated the then popular round arch, he rejected the robust, defensive-looking wall characteristic of many Richardsonian Romanesque houses of the period. The walls appeared more decorated than virile, and the clear trim lines underscored the basic planarity of these two facades. The principal material of the exterior was blue limestone; within, the hall was finished in oak without wainscoting, the parlor in Canadian maple, and both the dining room and library in cherry. Few architects have had the opportunity to design for one city so many essential buildings as McLaughlin did for Cincinnati. A partial list includes the old Court House, Widow's Home, Children's Home, Art Museum, City Opera, Masonic Hall, Public Library and several department stores, among them the famed Shillito store. He had already designed most of these when given the commission for the Laws house. He retired in 1912 and died in 1923. Unfortunately, this sturdy-looking structure has been demolished. (For Sheldon's description of the house, see the text.)

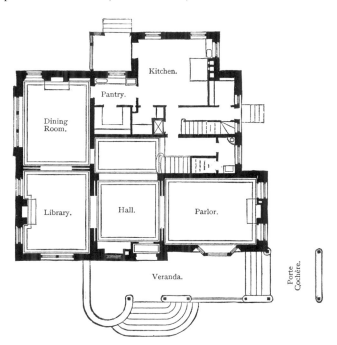

55. "Orchards," James H. Salisbury residence, Cleveland, O.; Charles F. Schweinfurth, architect, 1883–85. Salisbury (b. 1823) joined the faculty of the newly formed Charity Hospital Medical College in Cleveland in 1863. In addition to teaching and his private practice, he was active in research. Based on his studies, he recommended that problems of the digestive system should be treated with special diets and hot water. For his publications corroborating the germ theory of disease, Salisbury was recognized internationally. He specified for this house in the Glenville section of Cleveland a space for both his research and his practice. The arrangement of the ground floor reveals the challenge of separating family and professional activities within an integrated interior. Schweinfurth placed the office on the public side of the house, easily accessible from the front door. Presumably, patients could also wait in the vestibule of the hall. In order to protect the privacy of the family, the architect designed relatively narrow openings between all major spaces. Furthermore, he enabled the family to move from parlor to kitchen without entering the front hall. While the proximity of the stairway and office door was curious, the inhabitants of the house could also use the wide stairway adjacent to the dining room. It is reasonable to assume that Dr. Salisbury would not have approved of conveniences that might have harmed the health of his family. Apparently, he did not object to central heating; there were no grates in the sitting room or the office. The debate about the deleterious effects of central heating, particularly forced-air heating, was a lively one. Lewis Leeds, a writer on household technology, called it "the great curse of the American people. It is that dry, lifeless, withering, debilitating, poisoned stuff . . . which is filling our systems and warming and drying the life and substance out of about two-thirds of the people of this country." Conceivably, Salisbury could have requested the less common steam or hot water systems, but even then he would have disregarded the argument that numerous active grates were the only realistic means to counteract the stale, recycled air of central heating. Breathing impure air was a leading conversational topic of the decade. Designed in a mixed style, the Eastlake lathe work stands out from this vantage point. Clapboards covered the first floor and shingles the second. From 54'-high tower Canada could be seen across Lake Erie. Salisbury called his house the "Orchards" for the beautiful orchard which surrounded it, but it no longer exists today and the grounds are now part of an interstate access road. The cost of construction was approximately $12,000.

56. N. S. Possons residence, Cleveland, O.; Charles F. Schweinfurth, architect, ca. 1884. Sheldon referred to this house as "a modified Norman Shaw," a reference to the British architect whose country houses influenced American domestic design in the 1870s and early 1880s. The picturesque gabled roofs, textured surfaces, restricted applied ornament, concentrated windows, small panes and vernacular appearance were reminiscent of Shaw. On the other hand, Schweinfurth did not incorporate the half-timber work, high chimneys, unit composition or meandering ground plan that often characterized Shaw's work. The date of construction cannot be read on the shield of the carved wooden pediment; 1884 was the first year the family was listed at this address in the city directory. Today the house is gone and the site, 615 Case Avenue (E. 40th Street), is heavily industrialized. The elevation was oddly divided into two distinct parts: a brick first floor reflecting British tendencies and a two-story upper section that looked like a transplanted New England, shingle-style house. If the second and third stories suggest the country, the first reminds us that this was a house in a city. The brick wall, despite the projections of the stairway and dining room, was a barrier that could not be easily penetrated from the street, the windows were relatively high off the ground, the front door partially obscured, and the low but insistent iron railing clarified for passersby the line between the private and public territory of the lot. The size and centrality of the hall were not evident immediately, for the first feature seen after entering the modest front door was the side of the stairway, an arrangement unusual in this collection. Not until one rounded the corner could the hall and its focal point, a large fireplace that extended to the ceiling, be appreciated. The main-floor rooms were distinguished for their excellent woods: oak in the dining room, black walnut in the parlor and library, and cherry in the music room. In the shift from compartmentalized planning to the open plan, the spaces of the main floor in most houses became functionally less specialized and less individualized. Schweinfurth resisted the trend in this plan. A designated libarary and music room in the same house were not common. Furthermore, he created private spaces for the owners. In the basement was a remarkable laboratory where Possons, who in 1884 became a superintendent of the Brush Electric Company, conducted electrical experiments. In the attic was his billiard room and the studio in which Mrs. Possons painted the canvases that covered the walls of the first and second floors.

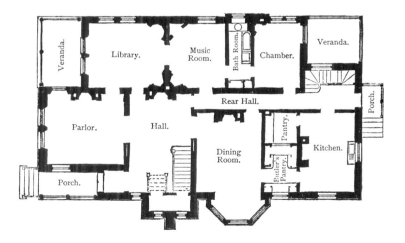

57. Albert Netter residence, Cincinnati, O.; James W. Mc-Laughlin, architect, 1881. The central portion of the first floor of the Netter house was reserved for reception and display, reflecting the importance of entertainment in the 1880s. As soon as guests walked through the front door into the mosaic-paved hall, they could see the carved stairway, centrally placed, covered by a domed ceiling and bathed in the soft light of a stained-glass window. Though impressive to visitors, such staged spaces were not essential to the family's daily routine. In numerous houses included in *Artistic Country-Seats*, the hall was treated as a space to live in, not simply one to admire or traverse. The resulting open plan could be formal, as in the Netter house, or informal, as in many of the resort cottages. Popular as open planning was, some critics objected. Wrote Louis H. Gibson, "This reception-hall idea, when carried to an extreme, has unprotected openings into a room which, merely for the purpose of designation, is named a library, or to other rooms, the openings to which are filled with ropes, strings, or spindle work, so that in fact there is only one great room on the main floor, other than the kitchen and dining-room. This is the extremest form of the reception hall, and it makes a second-floor sitting-room a necessity. It is an artificial development made possible by the class of people who are always abreast of the fads, and who operate from impulse rather than reason." Most critics regarded it as a natural consequence of central heating. As he did later in the Laws house (plate 54), McLaughlin tried to achieve compartmentalized and open planning simultaneously. Consistent with the taste of the period, the parlor was delicate, the library serious and the dining room elegant. The parlor was painted in soft colors, the library was finished in mahogany, while the ceiling of the dining room was ribbed and paneled and the wainscoting and cornice of the walls were done in cherry. Netter, an investment banker, built this house at 4 Oak Street, near the Reading Road, for $40,000. It no longer stands. McLaughlin chose a blue lime-stone, laid with controlled irregularity, for the exterior and red slate for the roof. The architect employed, with questionable success, varied gable profiles, pilasters and such eye-catching elements as the corner column of Bay of Fundy granite to hide a somewhat ponderous composition. Aware of the negative effects the downspout would have on a serious-looking facade, Mc-Laughlin tucked it into the right angle formed by two planes. He incorporated the metal gutter into the solid cornice to prevent it from detracting from the cornice's appearance.

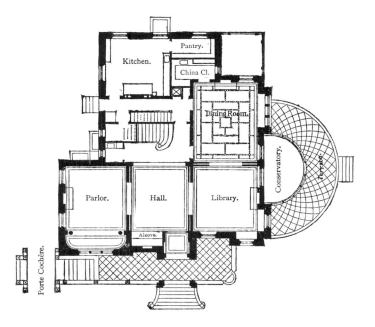

58. William Edgar residence, Newport, R.I.; McKim, Mead & White, architects, 1886. In his exemplary investigation of the evolution of the shingle style, Vincent Scully included numerous photographs from *Artistic Country-Seats* and frequently cited and interpreted Sheldon's remarks. He chose this photograph of the Edgar house as an example of the self-conscious quest for order that he documented in American architecture in the middle of the 1880s. His discussion of this house is perceptive: "It will not be possible here to trace the growth of a Renaissance or semi-classic type of design in the general work of McKim, Mead, and White and through them in American architecture as a whole. Notice should be taken, though, of the Commodore William Edgar House at Newport, 1885–86, where a stricter Georgian classicism began to invade their cottage architecture itself. Unlike the Appleton house [plate 15], in which the plan was still open and dynamic and where the new axial discipline was a supple and creative one, the Edgar House presents an interior space beginning to break up into boxes, losing something of flow while it searches for positive order. The central hall is arbitrarily tight in shape, and the subsidiary elements are quite symmetrically arranged. In both plan and elevation asymmetrical elements are introduced. Although these still freely express the varying functions of the different areas, they appear forced and out of place in relation to the whole. The varying shapes of the projecting bays of the exterior, as well as the variety of window sizes and placement, are examples in point. They are not integrated elements in a free organism but awkward elements in a rigid composition. The void of the porch over the drawing room is a welcome foil to the smooth solid brick of the service wing, but nothing unites the whole, and the scale again is uncertain. The point that may be grasped from this house is that a rigid, volumetrically fixed method was beginning to dom-inate McKim, Mead, and White's design." McKim, in charge of the project, used buff Roman brick with shingles on the roof. The dimensions are 117′ × 60′ and the cost was $42,870. Except for the loss of some woodwork, the house remains relatively unchanged at 29 Old Beach Road. The hall (27′ × 16′) was finished in oak, the morning or living room (18′ × 18′) in painted pine, the drawing room (20′ × 28′) with silk wall panels, the library (18′ × 16′) in cherry and the dining room (18′ × 28′) in American oak. Edgar (ca. 1810–1887) was the fourth generation of his pre-Revolutionary family named William. Known as "Commodore" because he had been Commodore of the New York Yacht Club for many years, he had been a summer resident of Newport since 1868.

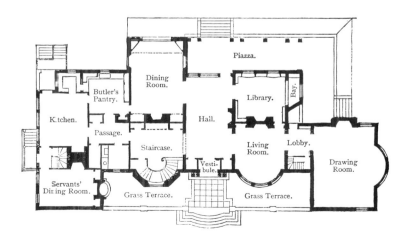

59. John H. Ammon residence, Cleveland, O.; Julius Schwein-furth, architect, 1881. This house stood at 1639 Euclid Avenue, a street Sheldon noted was "famed throughout the United States." Paved between 1873 and 1875 and lined with magnificent homes, it was a showplace of domestic architecture, particularly its "Millionaire's Row" between East 12th and East 40th Streets. It reached its apogee of social prominence in the 1880s and then gradually declined, in part, because the revolution in transportation—the horse-drawn trolley, the electric trolley (demonstrated in 1884 but not widely used in Cleveland before 1894) and the automobile—influenced the affluent families that had created the street to relocate in the suburbs. In its prime, however, Clevelanders compared Euclid favorably with the Unter den Linden of Berlin and the Champs-Élysées of Paris. This comparison is informative. Americans, confident, pleased and hungry for recognition, repeatedly pitted their achievements against those of Europe and invariably claimed equality or victory. Europeans, on the other hand, belittled the naïveté of these games of comparison. In effect, Americans believed that the new could be equal to the old and produced mansions to prove it. Admitting that end products could be copied, Europeans argued that mature theory required centuries of societal maturation. No local style, these expressive volumes, varied surfaces and numerous porches and verandas could be seen on suburban houses from the Midwest to New England. Articulated gables, bulbous, lathe-turned posts, corner brackets, varied rooflines and shingled projections were commonly found in houses of the Queen Anne movement. The slant of the property may have encouraged the placement of the kitchen in the basement. Entering from the porte-cochere, one evidently reached the hall from the basement, an unusual arrangement. Spacious but static, the rooms were relatively independent of each other. After serving in the infantry during the Civil War, Col. Ammon (1840–1904) opened a bookstore in Chicago, worked for publishers in New York and Boston, and for 17 years was head of the publishing department of Harper & Brothers. Two years before his death, he established the rare-book firm of Ammon and Mackell in New York. Because of travel obligations and the preference of his wife, Mary Josephine Saxton, a Cleveland native, the Ammons built their $20,000 home in Cleveland. Their library of more than 4,000 volumes was one of the largest private collections in the city. Schweinfurth (1858–1931) was a talented designer for Peabody and Stearns who joined his brother Charles in partnership in Cleveland from 1883 to 1884.

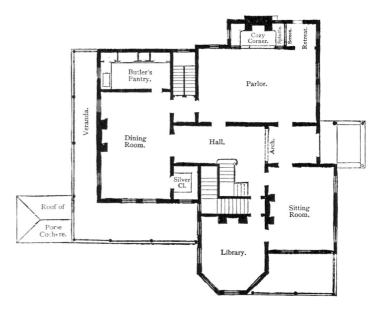

60. "Kelp Rock," Edmund C. Stedman residence, New Castle, N.H.; Edmund M. Wheelwright, architect, 1883. In his novel *Mrs. Peixada*, Henry Harland ("Sidney Luska") described the "indigenous" character of "Beacon Rock" or "Kelp Rock" as the house was known. "It looks as though it might have grown out of the soil; or as if the waters, in a mood of Titanic playfulness, had cast it up and left it where it stands upon the shore." His empathy for the uninhibited romanticism of the house was probably intended to please Stedman (1833–1908), one of the country's most influential literary critics. In addition to professorships at Johns Hopkins, Columbia and Pennsylvania, Stedman also wrote poetry, promoted poets and published numerous anthologies and critical studies. The structure probably cost less than the $25,000 it was estimated it would have cost if built at Newport or Long Branch. Local masons were used to set the white, dark and yellow coastal rocks into arbitrary patterns. Some shingles were dipped in oil and lampblack and others stained Venetian red. The tower (35' × 15') looked as if it had been reconstructed from the ruins of a lighthouse that had occupied the site for generations. Like romantics who risked death to stand heroically on some spectacular promontory, the family, living on the edge of this rocky coastline, could look nature in the eye and take its chances with fate. The hall was not a corridor but a living room with the great fireplace at one end and a constricted stairwell at the other. The kitchen and the piazza could be reached only through the dining room. From the platform in the middle of the stairs, one entered the study, possibly the space around which this summer retreat was conceived. It contained within its 2½'-thick walls colonial furniture, a cozy fireplace with crane and kettle, pictures (including two seascapes by Winslow Homer) and a recreational library. There were four bedrooms and a bath on the second floor and one bedroom above the study. A fragment of the house, the barely recognizable porch, still remains at the site on Wild Rose Lane.

In 1931 architect William L. White of Exeter, N.H. transformed "Kelp Rock" into an ampler and more restrained shingled house reflecting his period's disapproval of Wheelwright's romantic primitivism. Wheelwright (1854–1912) graduated from Harvard in 1876 and later studied architecture at M.I.T. and in Paris. After working for both Peabody and Stearns and McKim, Mead, and Bigelow, he formed his own office in 1883. An imaginative designer, he expressed himself in a profusion of styles. He served as city architect of Boston from 1891 to 1895 and published frequently, his best-known study being *School Architecture* of 1901.

61. Travis C. Van Buren residence, Tuxedo Park, N.Y.; Bruce Price, architect, 1886. Sheldon was intrigued by this cottage, calling it "the most original house by Mr. Bruce Price, and, in some respects, the most original in this country.... This originality consists partly in the effect of the portal, with its strong lights and shades.... Unquestionably, the eye of the spectator is detained by this very remarkable portal, and we shall look far and wide without finding its similitude either in manner of construction or in boldness of light and shade contrasts." Price designed a symmetrical facade in which attention is drawn strongly to the vertical axis of the steps, entrance, Palladian window and gable. The architect risked looking foolish by superimposing a hard, projecting window over a mobile, sensual opening. The rigidity of the "stuck-on" box was so unlike the suppleness of the cavity below. This contrast is dramatic enough to distract us from the skillful way in which he handled the rest of the elevation. By removing expected details from the surface, he reminds us of how much we take them for granted. Gone are the normal devices that separate one floor from another or call attention to the change in the direction of surface planes. The shingled hoods over the first-floor windows are barely perceptible. Even the gutters slant to the rear, leaving the envelope of shingles undisturbed. It is a textured skin that wraps, methodically but not inertly, around convincing interior volumes. This skin of shingles goes everywhere; at the compelling entrance it turns outside in, implying that interior walls are finished in the same manner. Without superb workmanship, this would have been impossible. The plan is a demonstration in creating symmetrical spaces and, like the exterior, is both simple and distinctive. It is a cruciform scheme with a major and a transverse axis. Although the identically shaped parlor and dining room represent geometric balance and order, spatially this collision of axes is dynamic. The strong fireplaces narrow the traffic lane, leaving one with the impression of passing through the center of an hour-glass, the space beyond seeming to be larger than it actually is. The hall, ample and centrally located, is less a hall than a sitting room, less a space to pass through than to reach. The kitchen is in the basement, possibly because Price believed this arrangement "encourages the servants to keep to themselves" and because of the restricted space on the main floor. Today the house is inhabited but it has been considerably altered. The shingled surface has been replaced with stucco and some half-timbered effects, the roof is slate, the Palladian window removed, and the front entrance now projects from the main wall. Van Buren, the brother of former President Martin Van Buren, paid about $10,000 for the house.

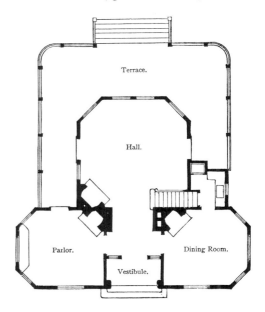

62. "Cottage G.," owned by Pierre Lorillard, J. L. Breese residence, Tuxedo Park, N.Y.; Bruce Price, architect, 1886. Tuxedo Park today is a commuter and retirement community of remarkable natural beauty that lies about 40 miles northwest of New York City. For several years during the 1880s it was the fall and winter capital of Eastern high society. It was created by the same wealth, expansiveness, confidence and pride that inspired the size, spatial freedom and opulence of so many houses in *Artistic Country-Seats*. In 1885 Pierre Lorillard V sold his rambling villa at Newport (plate 33) to Cornelius Vanderbilt. On September 18 of that year he took architect Bruce Price to a family tract in the Ramapo Hills and metaphorically waved his hand. By June of 1886, 5,000 acres had been fenced, 30 miles of roads graded, water and sewer systems laid, a 100-bed clubhouse completed, and several of the 40-odd houses and buildings designed by Price were ready for use. This was achieved by Price's creativity and hard work, the supervision of engineer Ernest Bowditch, 1,800 laborers imported from Italy and at least $1.5 million of Lorillard's money. On Memorial Day of 1886 Lorillard brought 700 selected guests from New York on three chartered trains to see the transformation and to sample the fruits of membership. According to Cleveland Amory, Lorillard developed a membership list that became a "guide to Who is especially Who in the Four Hundred." Intending at first to rent the cottages designed by Price, Lorillard decided to sell them to members of the Tuxedo Park Association; "Cottage G." was rented to J. L. Breese before his family decided to build their own house in the park. The colors of the exterior were keyed to the red of the brick chimney, and the allover color scheme of red and gray was intended to blend with the colors of the natural setting. As Samuel Graybill noted in his valuable study of Price, "Tuxedo looked old the day it was opened." Despite the setting and despite the preponderance of asymmetrical elevations in this series, "Cottage G." was from the lake side conscientiously symmetrical. It was dominated by the two massive chimneys, 40 feet high, which were invigorated by their pronounced entasis and which stood in opposition to the horizontality of the three floors slightly behind them. In addition to the obvious interplay of verticals and horizontals, Price also contrasted weight and lightness, roughness and smoothness, solids and cavities, and the graceful curves of chimneys, dormer, entrance and roof, with the precise cuts of the second story. Within, Price did not exploit the possibilities of open planning; there was no door between parlor and den. The cottage has been demolished. Breese, from a distinguished family of jurists, studied architecture and engineering and became an internationally respected amateur photographer.

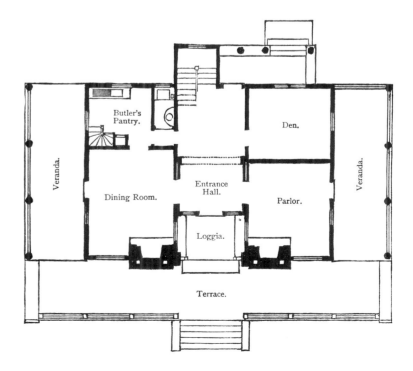

63. William Kent residence, Tuxedo Park, N.Y.; Bruce Price, architect, 1886. This skillfully designed $13,000 house was first owned by William Kent. Born in 1858, he studied law and became a member of the respected New York law firm of Tillotson & Kent. In 1881 he married Emily, the daughter of Pierre Lorillard. Price combined on the exterior traditional and formal elements with contemporary and vernacular ones. He acknowledged the natural setting through the gray traprock of the low platform wall and through the shingles that blended with the colors of the woods. The variations of light and shade on the shingles was similar to the effect of light on the bark of the trees. The gable was high, but its base, 40′ long, was broad enough to make its principal movement horizontal. While this gable was a decisive geometric form, lacking the entasis that made the gable of the Van Buren house (plate 61) appear more graceful, the rear of the house was softened by the undulating layers of shingles and the double curve of the roof. Price also included anachronistic elements. The band of decorative half-timber work owed more to the sixteenth and seventeenth centuries than to American trends of the 1880s. Fan windows were more common a century earlier and the corbels and columns supporting the porch roofs were features associated with the formal domestic architecture of the cities. The simple but effective cruciform plan provided light from three directions for each of the main rooms. The attic contained rooms for six servants whose working quarters were in the basement. The Kent house has been demolished. The remoteness of Tuxedo, although it made attracting and holding servants difficult, was one of the major reasons for its immediate appeal to the social community of New York. On October 15, 1886, the *Times* claimed that Tuxedo was taking over after Newport and Lenox had closed their seasons. On January 2, 1887, the paper reported that New York was losing the holiday social battle to country resorts, of which "Tuxedo has been the gayest and most attractive." This community offered members and visitors alike the advantages of English country life and American sports. Skating and ice boating became popular pastimes. At night tobogganers could shoot down an electrically illuminated slide to a point on the lake a half mile away, from which horse and cart returned them to the top of the hill. But there was another side to the woodsy informality. The dome of the clubhouse ballroom, 80′ in diameter, was supported on Corinthian columns. The club was staffed by English servants dressed in green uniforms with gold stripes. Members wore pins, an oakleaf on gold, but governors were identified by an acorn attached to the leaf.

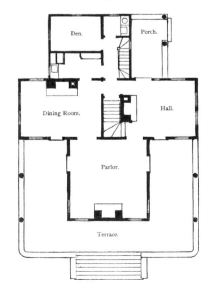

64. Henry I. Barbey residence, Tuxedo Park, N.Y.; Bruce Price, architect, 1886. The $18,000 Barbey house, one of the park's original cottages, did not last long, a victim of changing taste that rejected the idea of simple cottages in the woods for residences that marked the status of their owners more conspicuously. This outcome, almost predictable, stands in sharp contrast to the radical idealism of both Price and Lorillard in 1885 and 1886. Architect and client not only planned small houses but also houses that were stylistically off the beaten track. Sheldon observed, "Mr. Barbey's house is a genuine attraction of Tuxedo Park, with dimensions forty by sixty feet, and general effect extremely virile. . . . Mr. Price has taken special pains to avoid the long, lank, flat, crushed roof, although to get this result has been a labor." If the dominant expression of the Kent house (plate 63) was angularity, that of the Barbey house was rounded masses. Price rejected the traditional role and importance of edges by rounding the corners and bending and curving the roof lines. As Sheldon wisely noted, "It is easy enough to get rigidity, but it is difficult to get flexibility, in the exterior contours." Price also tapered the tower to complement the plasticity and the suppleness of the major section behind it. He pushed two basic parts together, a lower one that was strong and confident and a much larger upper one that appeared relatively lighter and more suspicious. Yet the strong stone was pink with speckles of quartz and topaz while the weaker shingles were stained a darker hue. The thick walls of the library and its isolation from the other rooms of the first floor suggest the compartmentalized planning of an English country house. The heavy fireplace of the elongated hall divided this space into two functional parts, the front serving as an intersection and the rear as the main sitting room. The plan fulfilled Price's seasonal requirements of the modern house: it "must be snug and comfortable, with broad hearth stones and warm walls to shield its tenants through the biting days of autumn and winter. The heat of summer demands shady porches and wide verandas." Probably because the house was not large, the kitchen was placed in the basement; however, the dining room was exceptionally spacious for these early Tuxedo cottages. Barbey (1832–1906), like most of the original 200 members of the Tuxedo Park community, was influential within New York business and social circles. He was a director of the Buffalo, Rochester & Pittsburg Railroad and of the Gallatin National Bank.

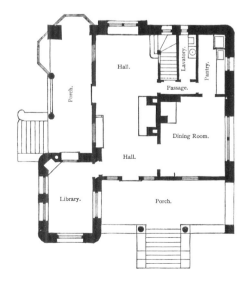

65. Pierre Lorillard, Jr. residence, Tuxedo Park, N.Y.; Bruce Price, architect, 1886. Despite the "eternal qualities" of buildings like the Parthenon which have impressed generation after generation, the "success" of most works of architecture is limited by changes in taste. Of this house Sheldon wrote, "How wonderfully harmonious it is, with all its details—how simple and yet how varied, having no incongruities, but winning the attention by straightforwardness and unity." Today this conclusion seems odd. Isn't this elevation full of incongruities? Samuel Graybill even asked if Price were playing games with his client, the son of Tuxedo's founder. The facade is broken by windows, varied in shape and placed arbitrarily. The large window at the upper right obscures the frieze. At the center Price gracelessly embedded a Palladian window in a Queen Anne tower and did not apologize for the friction between the Adamesque ornament and rough shingles. The entrance porch was inspired by one he had seen at Quogue, Long Island. How does one explain such a curious elevation? Perhaps he thought the dominant clapboards could overcome the obtrusiveness of disparate parts, perhaps the haste with which he worked in 1885 and 1886 at Tuxedo made uneven work inevitable, perhaps he took delight in combining old detail with new contexts, perhaps it was a conscious architectural response to the delicate balance of formality and informality that marked the etiquette of Tuxedo. Each of these explanations has its weakness. The fact remains that in most of his Tuxedo houses Price used powerful geometries to discipline unrefined surfaces, but here the power is gone and the surface, colonially inspired weatherboards, is quiet. In retrospect, this house may be prophetic. Houses built in the next quarter century at Tuxedo had more in common with the size and formality of this design than they did with those cottages that merged with the natural surroundings. The threatened unity of this design may also have reflected, unintentionally, the fragile position of this rural experiment in New York society. Intrigued but not entirely comfortable with Lorillard's planned community, New Yorkers eventually reaffirmed places like Newport and Bar Harbor. A sensation at first, dubbed by the *Times* as "that bright jewel of the Ramapo Valley," Tuxedo gradually lost its luster. Cleveland Amory recalled Julia Ward Howe's 1892 dismissal—"White of an egg." This original structure, approximately 75′ long and 30′ deep constructed for $14,000, remains on Tower Hill, though altered. Sheldon identified the owner as Pierre Lorillard, Jr., but it may have been owned by the Tuxedo Park Association, that is, Lorillard, Sr., until it was sold to Robert Fulton Cutting. Lorillard, Jr. built his own house higher on the hill.

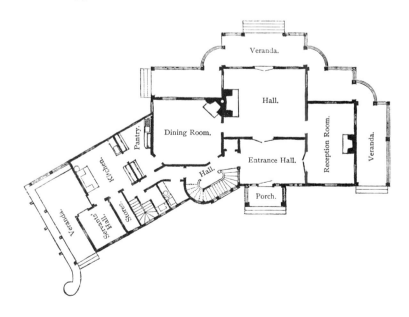

66. J. W. Johnson residence, Minneapolis, Minn.; Long and Kees, architects, 1884. Also known as the Johnson-Pillsbury house, this building was erected at 2200 Stevens Avenue South by a firm that erected major Minneapolis buildings in the Richardsonian Romanesque style in the late 1880s, among them the extant City Hall (begun in 1888) and Lumber Exchange building (1885) and the demolished Public Library building (1889). Franklin B. Long (1842–1912) and Frederick Kees (1852–1927) formed their partnership in the early 1880s. This house was constructed of white Kasota stone from the banks of the Minnesota River. Although nineteenth-century builders debated the advisability of seasoning stone just as they seasoned wood, Kasota stone was thought to be so firm and even that it could be set immediately after quarrying. However, the extended temperature range of Minneapolis took its toll on the Johnson house, requiring costly masonry repairs in 1912 and 1922 prior to its destruction in 1937. The First Christian Church now occupies the site. Sturdily composed, the exterior was modestly expressed with ornament of various periods. The ashlar walls were relieved by a Richardsonian Romanesque porch to the left, Renaissance references around the windows and at the roof level, and Gothic crenelation on the tower. Concerned that a barn-stable of wood might weaken the message of the $80,000 house—that an important family lives in it—the architects erected a $15,000 barn out of the same stone. The large plan (102' × 72') was mechanically conceived. Long and Kees first defined the L-shaped formal hall and the narrow rear hall, and then they located major rooms at the corners of this intersection. They chose mahogany for the hall and sitting room, bird's-eye maple for the parlor, cherry for the library and quartered oak for the dining room. The bedrooms were also finished in fine woods—two in cherry and two in quartered oak and one each in mahogany and sycamore. The remaining woodwork of this floor was exclusively brown ash. Each bedroom had a toilet-room and a fireplace. The bedroom fireplace was popular not only because it offered additional warmth in a cold climate but also because a grate fire was still considered one of the best means of minimizing the unwanted effects of central heating. "Furnace heaters constitute no complete system of ventilation: there is an influx of warm air, but no out-draught. The air becomes thickened," asserted an authority on healthy houses in *Lippincott's Magazine* of March, 1884. Indirect steam radiation, used in the Johnson house, was considered advanced for the day. Coils filled with steam warmed the air in several small chambers from which flues carried the heated air to the various rooms. Johnson (b. 1825) was a dry-goods merchant who gained control of the North Star Iron Works in 1874, and in 1881 became president of the City Bank in Minneapolis.

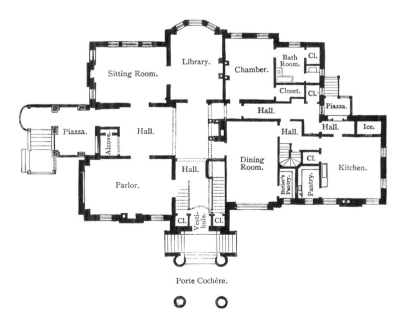

67. Erzelia F. Metcalfe residence, Buffalo, N.Y.; McKim, Mead & White, architects, 1884. Mrs. Metcalfe, widow of James H., once president of the First National Bank in Buffalo, commissioned this house in 1882 and moved into it in 1884 with her two sons, James S., then editor of the Modern Age Publishing Company, and George S., who worked for the same firm. Acknowledging the disparate sections of the exterior and the relatively undistinguished plan, Vincent Scully explained that it was not surprising that the three overworked partners and their numerous assistants sometimes failed to attain the firm's expected quality. The mediocre exterior and plan of the Metcalfe house could conceivably have been affected by conscious or unconscious sexism on the part of its architects. Sheldon, himself, admitted his prejudice against women clients and reported Henry H. Richardson's reservations about working with them. The exterior looked as if it had been put together by a committee, members of which requested equal time for their favorite material—local stone, red brick and shingles. Instead of a pleasing contrast between the rough-cut stone and the finished brick and shingles, the resulting collage, though eye-catching, was too discordant and loud. Against this cacophony of surfaces, the porte-cochere, well-crafted and delicate, looked miscast. Although in these years McKim, Mead & White usually made the hall the spatial and artistic heart of most of their houses, here it was located in the corner of the house and was poorly lighted. Although the library and dining room, joined by sliding doors, formed a unit which was ample and uncluttered, the dark staircase hall was largely consumed by the broad stairs that spilled into the middle of it. The inglenook seemed awkwardly placed and emphatically announced in this transitional space, and the parlor, tucked away behind the stairway, appeared to be an afterthought. Guests entering from the porte-cochere had the unusual choice of passing through the dining room or trespassing on servants' territory. Later, changes were made; the vestibule and small entryway were incorporated in the hall, and the parlor was connected to the back hall. Constructed at 125 West North Street for $23,500, the Metcalfe house is no longer standing. Despite the shouts of preservationists, it was demolished in 1980; however, the entry, vestibule, staircase hall, back hall and parlor were obtained by the Metropolitan Museum in New York for possible inclusion in Phase II of the New American wing. If the heart of this section is installed, the public will have an opportunity to examine the fine finish of the interior, specifically, the hall of quartered oak with its fireplace of Siena marble below, carving and beveled glass mirror above, and the screen of delicate balusters at the side.

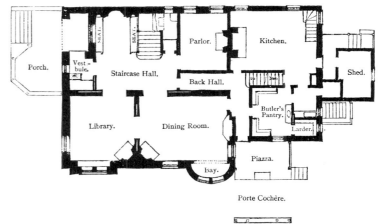

68. Elizabeth L. Milbank risidence, Greenwich, Conn.; Lamb and Rich, architects, 1886. Reflecting national tendencies in the 1880s, the Milbank house was marked by significant inconsistencies. The character of the outside of this residence was unlike that of the inside, and neither corresponded in spirit to the means that made living there a comfortable, convenient experience. Granted, the exterior was eclectic like the interior. It was Queen Anne in its plasticity and Renaissance, Romanesque and Gothic in its detail. The mosaic floor of the spacious piazza was patterned after Roman work. However, the dominant message of the exterior was power. Charles Rich, the principal designer, who could be picturesque in wood, was here ruggedly sculptural and tactile in stone and tile. However, evidence of such crude, even eccentric, strength was absent within. The hall, for example, was wainscoted from floor to ceiling with panels carved with Renaissance details, a wrought-iron grille from Florence protected the lemon glass window (19′ × 10′) of the stairway, and the fireplace to the right included cherubs after Luca della Robbia warming their hands. The walls of the vast parlor (24′ × 44′) were covered with Japanese embroidery, the ceiling was bamboo and the woodwork was lacquered a deep red. The library was quietly finished in gumwood and the dining room in mahogany. In effect, the interior was a composite of expensive historical and cultural references. If the Milbank house looked like a fortress from the street and a reminder of a Cook's tour within, its technology was unrelated to either. Such inconsistencies may pain some twentieth-century critics, but they did not trouble architects and clients of the 1880s. Like most middle- and upper-class dwellings, this house offered mechanical conveniences unprecedented in the history of domestic architecture. There were overhead flush toilets, central heating and hot and cold running water. The house also contained a rare elevator. How could Rich embrace these new devices and for the same structure design medieval crenelation on the outside and a bamboo ceiling on the inside? The kind of unity implied by the question was not a major consideration. This was "go-ahead"—if not "go-as-you-please"—architecture, an architecture saved from failure or laughter by the very vitality that made these discontin-

uities so blatant. Elizabeth Lake Milbank was the widow of Jeremiah, who died in 1884 leaving $32 million. She gave a library to Greenwich and was once the most generous contributor to Barnard College. In 1857 Jeremiah formed a company with Gail Borden, a Texan searching for money to finance a condensed-milk business. In 1919 the firm was renamed the Borden Company. Milbank also founded the Chicago, Milwaukee and St. Paul Railroad in 1863. The house, at East Putnam and Milbank Avenues, was razed in 1955.

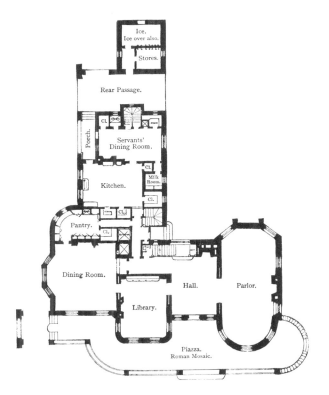

69. William H. Scott residence, Philadelphia, Pa.; George T. Pearson, architect, 1886. After the usual protests by preservationists, historians and lovers of architecture, this firm, crisp house was regrettably demolished in the early 1970s. As a footnote to its existence and history, the stone wall and entrance gates, deprived of their concrete spheres, remain in front of the federally subsidized housing unit now standing on this site at School House Lane and Wayne Avenue in Germantown. Sheldon anticipated a bright future for American architecture but, unsure of identifying the Scott house as a "suburban cottage" or a "villa" and admitting that its style could not be easily classified, granted that this residence was not proof that the golden day had arrived. Yet he congratulated Pearson for answering special requirements, particularly the family's demand for privacy on a public street. Unlike the large majority of houses included in *Artistic Country-Seats*, the main veranda of the house was not placed on the street side (School House Lane) where members of the family could see and be seen but, together with the library and dining room, at the rear. Undoubtedly, the front porches of this series were encouraged by the atmosphere that prevailed at resorts or in the country and by the protection afforded by spacious surroundings of suburban estates, but they were also common in residential districts, even when these special conditions were missing. If exposed verandas were signs of the faith of owners in their social environment, the Scott house could be interpreted as a questioning of that confidence. The stone wall, rare in this series, anticipated the "defensible space" articulated by Oscar Newman in 1972. It was a barrier that did not obstruct views of the residence but did discourage passersby from crossing it. The stones projecting from the top were as threatening as they were decorative. Although this wall was broken in places to permit access to the front door, these gaps were treated so emphatically that one passing through the portal was immediately aware of having entered a special domain re-

quiring special conduct. Finally, hard, formal and businesslike, the front porch did not encourage loitering by the uninvited. The cost of the house, wall and stone stable was approximately $25,000. Gray stone was used for the walls, red tiles for the roof, and glazed brown tiles in the gable ends. Pearson (1847–1920) was born in Trenton, N.J., worked for John McArthur and Addison Hutton in Philadelphia, and opened his own office there in 1880. Much of his work was executed in the Germantown region. Scott was a founding partner of the printing house of Allen, Lane & Scott, one of Philadelphia's largest and most prestigious. Also a civic leader, he sat on the boards of hospitals and charitable agencies.

70. "Druim Moir," Henry H. Houston residence, Philadelphia, Pa.; W. D. and G. W. Hewitt, architects, 1886. Houston (1820–1895) was probably the largest private landowner in Philadelphia in the 1880s, having accumulated his wealth through the Pennsylvania Railroad, shipping, petroleum, and gold mines in the West. Co-operatively, the Pennsylvania built a line through his extensive holdings on the west side of Chestnut Hill known as Wissahickon Heights, enabling the residents of his planned community to commute to the city. By the end of the decade Houston had commissioned over 80 houses; "there was no ticky-tacky in Wissahickon Heights," observed Richard Webster. Houston also shaped the social climate by hiring the Hewitts to design the roomy Wissahickon Inn and subsidizing the move of the Philadelphia Cricket Club to the community in 1883. This "old-country" flavor was also reflected in the name of his house, "Druim Moir," meaning great ridge, a well-fortified area of County Down in Ireland. For many years the headquarters of the Houston Foundation, this somewhat altered structure at the corner of Willow Grove Avenue and Cherokee Street will be turned into condominiums. One of the largest residences of this suburb, it cost approximately $115,000 when completed in July, 1886 ("1885" is worked into the decoration of the oriel). Despite the mixed style, the intended impression was that of an English country estate. The architects chose Chestnut Hill gray stone for the walls, Eastern granite for the trim, and shingles for the roof, producing a massive form, long and high (the top of the five-story tower has been removed), which bursts frequently into plastic exclamations and which is wrapped in a nervous rock-faced skin. The layers of stone, the voussoirs of the windows and arches, the granite sills and the articulation of the courses have been incorporated skillfully. From a twentieth-century vantage point, we may question its spatial overkill in meeting the needs of a single family or the apparent inconsistency of an enterprising capitalist preferring such an artistically conservative statement, but we cannot deny that its designers and work-men believed that every square foot of its elevation was important or that they understood architecture to be an expressive medium. If the functional sectioning of the interior was somewhat out of step with the increasing flexibility of the mid-1880s, the effort, though somewhat awkwardly expressed, to push the walls of certain rooms into space was not. The interior is notable for the variety of woods employed: oak for the hall and stairway, butternut for the parlor, mahogany for the reception room, quartered oak in both library and dining room, sycamore for the office and cypress for the servants' section. Oak, cherry and sycamore were chosen for the bedrooms of the second floor and pine for those of the third.

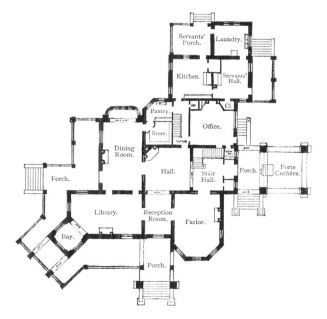

71. J. M. Wayne Neff residence, Cincinnati, O.; Bruce Price, architect, 1882. Neff was president of the Arctic Ice Machine Manufacturing Company in Cincinnati. Members of the Neff family rented cottages at Bar Harbor, where Price also vacationed, possibly accounting for this commission. Within *Artistic Country-Seats*, this was the earliest of the eight houses designed by Price. He built the foundation and terraces of stone, used half-timber work in the gable and the upper tower and covered the remainder of the surfaces and the roof with wooden shingles. Compared to his tendencies in the later houses at Tuxedo Park, this exterior was more complicated and the interior more fluid. The composition was anchored by the fat tower, partially hidden behind the foreground trees, which was supported to either side by dissimilar gables. The designer utilized the substance of the powerful tower to accentuate the voids of the veranda and sleeping porches. Although he often employed shingles at Tuxedo Park as an unbroken skin holding the interior pressures in check, here the exterior appears to be composed of numerous forms, each of them distinctive, that have been jammed together. The result is a complex piece of architectural sculpture, one that obscures the nature of the space within. As he varied the materials of the surfaces, he also chose motifs eclectically. The tower reflected Norman architecture; the chimneys and half-timber work, English architecture of the fifteenth and sixteenth centuries; and the screens of the rear porch, Japanese work. The two-sided veranda permitted the family public exposure and privacy in this suburban neighborhood. The plan was a fine example of a large hall that functioned as the hub of the house laterally and vertically. Standing within this darker area, one would be attracted from several directions by the light entering the bay and circular windows of adjacent rooms. Although the spatial movement into surrounding rooms was encouraged, Price first attracted the attention of those coming

through the front door with the heavily carved fireplace and mantel, the decorative panels of which continued to the ceiling. Then the stairway, which required multiple changes of direction as it rose around its throne-like seat, was discovered and, finally, the entrances into adjacent rooms. This hall was wainscoted in oak, the parlor finished in a Louis XIV style, and the library and dining room done in cherry. Constructed for approximately $25,000, the Neff house stood at the corner of Reading Road and Oak Street but has been demolished.

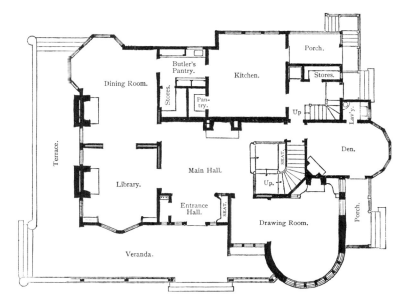

72. "Fair Oaks," William D. Washburn residence, Minneapolis, Minn.; E. Townsend Mix, architect, 1883. "Fair Oaks," whose 90′ tower dwarfed all surrounding flora, was once the most impressive domestic palace in Minneapolis. The estate, at Stevens Avenue and 24th Street, was reportedly worth $750,000 in the mid-1880s, the value significantly affected by its ten-acre park (Fair Oaks Park today) laid out by Frederick Law Olmsted. Washburn (b. 1831) moved from Maine to Minnesota in 1857 to practice law but quickly became successful in lumber, flour and railroads. He served as a state representative in Washington from 1879 to 1885 and as senator from 1889 to 1895. The house (120′ × 116′) was constructed of Kasota stone in a nineteenth-century Gothic idiom. Mix compensated for the relatively restrained lower stories by overloading the roof with strongly profiled masses. Inside, the house was sumptuously finished; mechanically, it was one of the most advanced Sheldon included. To make things clear at the threshold, Mix covered the vestibule's floor with mosaic, its walls with marble wainscoting and its ceiling with frescoes. Then came a magnificent axis, a domestic nave that terminated in the high altar of the dining room. Its coved and ribbed ceiling was 14′ high and its walls were finished in heavy stamped leather. Even larger was the drawing room (22′ × 38′), executed in a light Louis XIV style with walls covered with tapestry silks, a mantel of onyx, and inlaid and gilt rosewood woodwork. For family gatherings, the Washburns preferred the 18′ × 30′ living room of Santo Domingo mahogany. The dark library was done in wood imported from Austria. Tales of steps Americans were willing to take to make their houses comfortable were met in Europe with a mixture of contempt, curiosity and respect. If some critics abroad charged that gadgetry was alien to "a man's castle," others claimed that the Americans were taking the lead in applying technology to make homes healthier. The Washburn house, certainly no artistic pacesetter, probably set local standards for convenience through labor-saving devices. The plumbing system alone cost $20,000;

almost all of the 14 bedrooms (the Washburns had six children) had attached toilets and bathrooms. The house was lighted by electricity and warmed indirectly by steam. After dinner the men could ride the elevator directly to the billiard room. Their cigar smoke could be removed in 20 minutes from any part of the house through a ventilating system hidden in the roof. Unfortunately, the next generation could not afford to keep up this splendor. Occupied for years by a caretaker, the house became a servicemen's center run by the Girl's Liberty League in the First World War, and in 1924 the Minneapolis Park Board voted to raze it. Mix (1831–1890), an established architect of Milwaukee since 1856, was appointed state architect of Wisconsin in 1874. His most important building in Minneapolis was the Metropolitan Building (1884–89), no longer extant.

73. Charles F. Brush residence, Cleveland, O.; George H. Smith, architect, 1884. In 1881 France named Brush (1849–1929) a Chevalier de la Légion d'Honneur for his pioneering work in making the arc lamp practical and in developing power stations to illuminate it effectively. When the first urban demonstration of the "Brush system" was held on Cleveland's Public Square in 1879, "a dazzling glory filled the park." Before the end of the 1880s the Brush Co. made over $2 million in profits by providing streetlights for New York, Boston, Philadelphia, Baltimore, Montreal, Buffalo and San Francisco. Brush obtained power for his backyard laboratory and for 400 incandescent lights in his house and grounds through a windmill, 45′ in diameter. The structure shown at the rear of the house in the photograph may be a portion of this windmill. The house, set back 300′ from Euclid Avenue, was built in 1884 and torn down after Brush's death, as he requested in his will. One of the stateliest houses in the series and hardly a "country seat," the lower portions were based on Italian Renaissance sources while the attic floor and towers are closer to the Northern Renaissance. It was finished in a sandstone widely used in Cleveland and throughout the eastern part of the country, a buff Amherst stone that darkened with age. Neither plan nor elevation convey the size of the Brush house. The Euclid facade was 96′ wide, the east elevation 140′ and the tower, 14′ in diameter at the base, was 80′ high. The scale of specific rooms and the exquisiteness of their finish stand out as the distinguishing features of the interior. The main part of the hall, for example, was clad in mahogany from the floor to the base of the attic. At the rear of this 16′ × 50′ space was a stairway of dark mahogany with balusters and ornaments of bronze, with a stained-glass window on the main landing as the principal source of light. The aluminum ceiling was painted in a pattern of warm colors. The rosewood library was 42′ × 20′ and the dining room, in English oak with a coved ceiling containing a stained-glass skylight, measured 31′ × 28′. It is conceivable,

then, that a guest might have to walk almost 70′ from the library before being able to sit down to eat. The largest space, however, was the third-floor ballroom, 55′ × 35′, with wainscoting and heavy rafters of oak. The flexible, open planning found in many suburban and resort houses was replaced here by a plan that formalized and didactically isolated every family function. Mr. B. had his room and Mrs. B. hers; one dined in the dining room and made pastries in the pastry room. The architect was George H. Smith (1849–1924), who designed several important buildings in Cleveland: the Hickox (1890), the Rose (1900), the Colonial Arcade (1898) and, with John Eisenmann, the world-famous Arcade (1890).

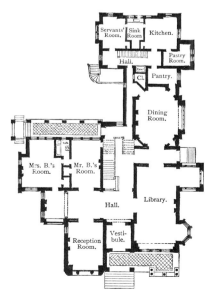

74. "Rock Gate," Lucius A. Barbour residence, Washington, Conn.; Rossiter and Wright, architects, ca. 1885. Named for the outcropping of stone circled by the driveway, this $22,000 house overlooking the Shepaug Valley is still occupied. The firm built several houses here, and Ehrick K. Rossiter (1854–1941), the principal designer, retired to this region in about 1931. Born in Paris of an artistic family, he graduated from Cornell, returned to Europe for two more years of study, and in 1877 established his office in New York City, where he handled mainly domestic work. The photograph shows the north side of this frame house which was covered with rough pine shingles stained brown with trimmings of cream. In 1882 Rossiter published *Modern House Painting*; its fine colored plates in ochre, chocolate, dark olive, rust, sand and pale orange in three-, four-, and five-color systems demonstrated the importance he attached to color and his sensitivity in handling it. In this book, he asserted that "the new school of designers was, and is now, eclectic, claiming the right to use the special features and details of any and every style, which can be bent to harmonize with the requirements of their buildings." Such eclecticism could be risky, but Rossiter could afford to experiment because he was a fine composer. In the Barbour house he added his accents— clean and light circles and rectangular panels—gently. He was able to indulge his antiquarian bent without marring the contemporary appearance of the house because he knew how to use such elements unpretentiously. The cream horizontal trim foreshadowed Frank Lloyd Wright's broken horizontals of the prairie houses, but Rossiter's purpose differed. Here the white lines were employed to add movement without compromising the integrity of the mass, to lead the eye around the house and not, as in Wright's work, to articulate abstract planes of an architectural collage. For

example, the parallel lines at the base of the second floor pull together the circular alcove, the dark entranceway and the projecting staircase block. The visitor is drawn into the darkness of the porch and then, once inside, attracted by the openness and light of the circular parlor and piazza. Rossiter also contrasted his interior spaces creatively—the public area of the hall with the more intimate nook, and the white parlor with the redwood den. Barbour was a manufacturer of spool cotton who was born in Indiana in 1846 but moved to Hartford, Connecticut as a child. In 1882 he became associated with the Willimantic Linen Co., which at that time employed 2,000 workers. Subsequently, he became a partner in H. C. Judd & Root, wool commission merchants.

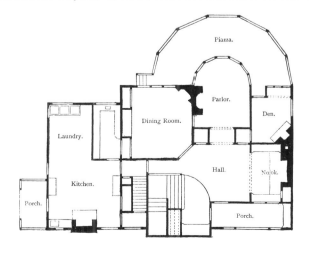

75. "Torworth," Justus C. Strawbridge residence, Philadelphia, Pa.; Addison Hutton, architect, 1885. According to Elizabeth Yarnell, who wrote a biography of her grandfather, Addison Hutton, in 1974, this house was first built as a two-story Georgian residence. To the block of the original building, Hutton added a third floor and a loft and on the north side a porte-cochere, tower and several rooms. Although these additions were incorporated satisfactorily—one of the children of Strawbridge remembered that the result "was to us a very attractive home"—it is possible to detect the Georgian structure in both plan and elevation. In all likelihood, the plan of the former house was symmetrical, a central hallway with two rooms to either side, and did not contain the servants' work spaces to the rear. The dotted lines, references to arched screens of wood, mark the location of the former walls. In the original construction the square perimeter of this section was conceived first and the rectangular rooms within it second. The new rooms on the north side—the antehall, study and dining room—were conceived as artistic shapes whose exterior forms would add fashionable picturesqueness to the formerly fashionable orderliness of the first structure. Without destroying the bilateral symmetry of the principal front, Hutton added as a focal point a central gable, oddly supported by an octagonal bay which in turn rests disquietingly on the porch roof. To connect the surfaces of the two sections, the brick walls were covered with wet plaster against which pebbles were thrown, producing a "pebbledashed" finish. Nevertheless, some specific features of this enlargement look awkward or strange. Both the pavilion and the porte-cochere appear to be afterthoughts. Where is the missing room that would incorporate the lonely chimney to the north? The wide, inviting porch offers no doors. The size of the house is greater than we may judge it to be—85′ wide and 128′ deep. Likewise, the rooms are larger than the plan implies: the oak-finished antehall (17′ in diameter), the main hall, also in oak (32′ × 27′), the dining room in red oak (32′ × 16′), the study in light walnut (23′ × 16′), the reception parlor in buff-enameled pine

(27′ × 18′), the drawing room in dark mahogany (37′ × 17′) and the library, also in dark mahogany (27′ × 15′). "Torworth," at the corner of School House Lane and Wissahickon Avenue in Germantown, was converted into the Alden Park Inn, which was destroyed by fire in May, 1979. In the introduction to Yarnell's study, George Tatum refers to Hutton as a "Quaker architect," a Quaker who built for Quaker clients. One of them was Justus Strawbridge (1838–1911), merchant, financier and a leading citizen of Philadelphia. From a different branch of that city's Quakers than his dry-goods partner, Isaac Clothier, Strawbridge became a benefactor of Haverford College while Clothier contributed heavily to Swarthmore.

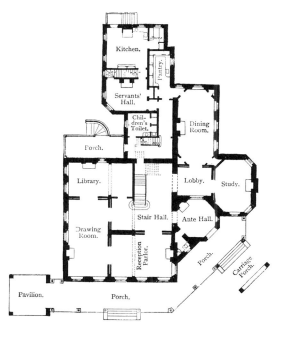

76. H. Victor Newcomb residence, Elberon, N.J.; McKim, Mead & White, architects, 1880. Twentieth-century historians have considered this house a brilliant example of the emerging shingle style and evidence of McKim, Mead & White "at their original best." Critics and architects of the late nineteenth century also recognized its importance in the evolution of American domestic architecture. It was one of the few buildings included by Appleton and Co. in both *Artistic Country-Seats* and *Artistic Houses* of 1883–84. Architect Bruce Price considered it the forerunner of "the type of shingle houses that have since become so distinctively an American class." Mariana van Rensselaer thought it the best of the firm's work in the Long Branch area because it was integrated so well with the site. "It looks as though it stood firmly on its feet, as though it were rooted and grounded, as though it had *grown*, while too many of our seaside houses look as though they had not even been built in place, rather, as though they had been dropped down ready-made by accident." The house did sit comfortably on its site, spreading out unhurriedly and acquisitively as it consumed more than enough ground for the summer needs of a single family and its friends. Its dimensions and spacious lawn were reminders of wealth, but the way this wealth was expressed was new. This summer palace was more expansive than overwhelming, more informal than impressive. The typical means of expressing social power through architecture—formal composition, thick walls, fine materials, proven styles—have not been employed. The confidence of McKim, Mead & White is evident in the way they have casually thrown together odd, distinctive forms that have not ruined the unity of the design. The thrown-together look of the plan may obscure the firm's genius in creating spaces that flow together and spread outward. This phenomenon could be understood best when standing in the large hall. Here one was in the hub of the house, an ample area that seemed to push surrounding spaces to the very edge of the plan. Between the hall and the bays and the hall and drawing room were White's exquisite wooden screens suspended from the ceiling. Although these defined the hall, the light and space seen through them also implied the continuation of the hall beyond its geometric perimeter. Built for approximately $33,000, the house, whose present address is 1265 Ocean Avenue, was changed in 1946 into a one-and-a-half-story, symmetrically composed structure initially finished in stucco and later in brick. Its magnificent lawn remains. Newcomb was born in Louisville in 1844. He succeeded his father as head of the Louisville & Nashville R.R. and then, about 1880, went to New York, where he established the U.S. National Bank. He became mentally ill in 1890 and died in 1911.

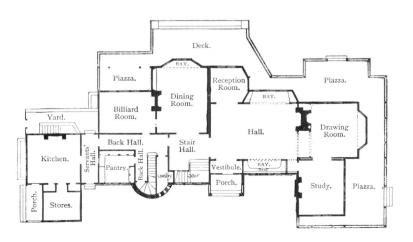

77. George Noakes residence, New York, N.Y.; Arthur B. Jennings, architect, 1884. Despite its granite, this house on Riverside Drive between West 113th and West 114th Streets stood for only 22 years, from 1884 to 1906. Its brief existence reveals the vulnerability of late nineteenth-century American architecture in the face of rapid urban development. Owners were prepared to spend considerable sums of money to obtain, as soon as possible, spacious and carefully finished residences but evidently did not consider that the same forces that made such mansions possible would eventually threaten their existence. To Noakes and Jennings this residence was proof of means and artistic skill; to those who ordered its destruction in 1906 it had become an obstruction to "progress." Jennings combined features of English Victorian architecture with the round arch and strength of the modern Romanesque. He apparently planned to use a particular quarried stone but was urged to visit another quarry where he found granite paving blocks, more attractive in color and cheaper than ordinary varieties of stone. He ordered the blocks, trimmed them slightly and laid them in a random ashlar pattern. Characteristic of his compositional inclinations, the main face became plastically vigorous at the second level. Although the textured stone and the natural revelation of internal functions could have carried the artistic responsibilities, Jennings preferred to add the corbeled tower (oriel window) and the two corbeled windows, all three of which looked more applied than integral, and contrasted their projecting forms with the darker voids. On the other hand, these lookouts offered the family and friends excellent views of the Hudson River. The plan of this house was odd. Basically a rectangle, it bore little relationship to the complicated geometries of the main facade. The diamond-shaped hall, placed in the center,

would have been very dark if Jennings had not included wide windows at the landing of the stairway. This landing, originally planned to hold an organ, was large enough to serve as a sitting room. Because of the hall's unique shape, the shape and corners of the vestibule and library were awkward. The architect's segmental, arbitrary approach to planning is also evident in the octagonal dining room. There were stronger reasons for his placement of the 18′-high conservatory near the water supply of the kitchen and the secluded sewing room from which Mrs. Noakes managed the domestic staff. The floors of better urban houses were finished in hardwoods in the 1880s. The Noakes floors were built with a system of three layers, the first of grooved pine or hemlock, the second of thick paper and the top layer of hard wood.

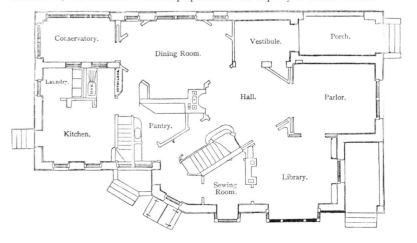

78. Elberon Casino, Elberon, N.J.; Peabody and Stearns, architects, 1883. Until it was removed in 1959, the Casino stood near the juncture of Lincoln and Elberon Avenues. The lawns of the better cottages along this flat coastal region were exceptionally fine, as is evident in the grounds surrounding the club. A garden hose stands rolled at the corner of the porte-cochere. Unlike Newport, where nonmembers and blue-collar workers reportedly mixed inside the casino, the Elberon Club was planned as a sanctuary for acceptable people. It was incorporated in 1882 by eight men who were listed in the Social Register as a means of coping with the influx of undesirables. The very fashionable cottagers at Elberon were threatened by the large, heterogeneous summer crowd at Long Branch immediately to the north. The casino, essentially a resort country club, was a new type of architecture that appeared in the late 1870s and early 1880s. In addition to the casino at Elberon, Sheldon included photographs of three other casinos: Newport (plates 16, 17), Short Hills (plate 26) and Narragansett Pier (plate 52). Although the members of the Elberon Club may have owned one residence in New York or Philadelphia and a country house in addition to their seaside cottage in Elberon, their casino or social headquarters was surprisingly modest and inexpensive to build ($17,725). Perhaps we should not be surprised since this was also true of many of the summer cottages owned by the members of the casino, though not true of their winter club in the city. For summer use, however, it was architecture appropriately roomy and informal, and its vast living room and functional theater served both spontaneous and organized social activities. Critics have written positively about this building. Sheldon noted that its sparse decoration called attention to its simplicity and pleasing distribution of masses. Vincent Scully described the building as "a loose, picturesque assortment of shingled shapes which flow together in massing like the waves of the sea.... The building's greatest quality is its free virtuosity in wood frame construction and the unification of that variety by the continuous shingled surface." In December, 1886 *The Builder* of London considered it "an example of what may be called the new American school of domestic architecture, which is striking out a form and feeling of its own." From the British perspective, "form" meant undecorated, horizontally oriented houses of wood and "feeling" meant their unpretentious and informal character. Though this long building is clearly an artistic unit, the portion to the right of the porte-cochere differs in character from the section to the left. It is slower in pace, less broken, and more expressive of internal volumes than the flat planes and cleanly cut openings of the other side.

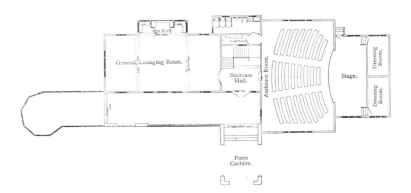

79. Rufus C. Jefferson residence, St. Paul, Minn.; George Wirth, architect, 1884. Visually attractive, a well-designed house could also suggest the ways in which its owners wished to be understood by the public. For example, a passerby could imagine a family behind a Queen Anne front as being spirited and open-minded, one behind a Richardson Romanesque facade as being socially reserved but strong-willed, and the family within this house, defined by Sheldon as "modern Renaissance, sometimes called modern French," as one that sought respectability or possessed genuine class. It was commissioned by Rufus Jefferson, whose considerable wealth was obtained through lumber, real estate and farm loans. Born in Gainsville, N.Y. in 1843, he settled in St. Paul in the early 1880s. His firm of Jefferson and Kasson owned one of the largest lumber stands in the state. Overlooking downtown St. Paul at 276 Summit Avenue on a lot 400′ by 175′, the house, torn down in 1930, cost approximately $75,000 before the decorators moved in. Sheldon wrote an informative description of the hall and parlor. "You enter the tiled porch into a tiled vestibule, wainscoted in oak to the frescoed ceiling, and thence into the large hall, which is the principal feature of the interior. Opposite the vestibule, the large fireplace is tiled from top to bottom, and furnished with wrought-iron fire-dogs, baskets, and so on, and with an over-mantel of oak, set with mirrors of various sizes, of beveled glass. The hall is finished in antique oak, wainscoted six feet high, and the wall-spaces have tapestry hangings whose prevailing tint is olive-green, representing forest scenes, while the ceiling is paneled with stucco moldings, bronzed and frescoed. To the left, the parlor, finished in dark mahogany, but without wainscot, has wall-spaces hung in golden silk tapestry in the lower part, with a frieze of bluish plush, hand painted. The mantel has a facing of Low's art tiles, very expensive, and its principal part is supported by two Ionic columns of mahogany, nine feet high, carrying a heavy carved cornice of mahogany. Above the shelf appears a large mirror, framed in mahogany, and the ceiling is tinted very lightly. The *portieres* of tapestry, in hand-worked

panels, represent ladies in old costumes, one panel alone costing over two hundred dollars." Wirth selected cherry for the library, white oak for the dining room and modest white pine for the parlor. Though treated simply, the eight bedrooms were finished in hardwoods while Jefferson's studio on the third floor was pine stained dark. The exterior was primarily pressed red brick with trim in light sandstone and the friezes in terra-cotta. Wirth was born in Bavaria in 1851, arrived in the United States in 1869, and entered Cornell University as a special architectural student in 1876. He opened his office in St. Paul in 1879.

80. James Adams residence, Buffalo, N.Y.; Green and Wicks, architects, 1882. This house was commissioned by one of Buffalo's more active and successful businessmen of the 1880s. He was born in Martha's Vineyard in 1823, but his family settled in Buffalo when he was ten. By the age of 31, he was the owner and manager of a tobacco-processing factory. Typical of the many individuals who made extraordinary fortunes in these years, Adams was no specialist, for he was active in lumber, railroads and utilities. At the time his house was being built, he was the principal partner of Adams, Moulton and Company, one of the most important lumber dealers in the state, and shortly after *Artistic Country-Seats* was published he became vice-president of the Brush Electric Co. in Buffalo. Since Adams was a timber magnate, it is understandable that his house was constructed, at least in part, of wood. However, as the plates of this publication verify, the business leaders of the cities of the "Northwest," cities like Buffalo, Cleveland, Minneapolis and St. Paul, clearly preferred to live in houses of stone or brick despite the widespread use of wood in country and resort architecture. As the decade progressed, the use of wood in city residences declined and, increasingly, members of respectable urban circles viewed wood as a material that was too common, tentative and dangerous. Assuming that Adams was faced with a difficult decision, Green and Wicks resolved his "dilemma" creatively. They placed a "fragile" top on a solid-looking base of brownstone and pressed brick and treated the chimneys as disciplinarians to keep the upper stories in check. This solution gives us a rare opportunity in this publication to see the shingle style west of the Alleghenies. The architects did not wrap the house in shingles in the manner of Bruce Price, and they did not stretch them across broad planes as W. R. Emerson might have done. Instead, the shingled sections serve as links between functional forms that catch our eye, such as the paneled gable, the chimneys and the octagonal bay. Although the house is still standing at 17 Tudor Place and its major masses, porches, dormers and bays are intact, the carved panels have disappeared and the shin-gled surfaces are now half-timbered. The exterior was a relatively expressive interpretation of a relatively inexpressive interior. The architects seem to have created the plan in two stages, first starting with a basic Georgian arrangement and then doctoring it to avoid monotony. Edward B. Green (ca. 1856–1950) and William Sydney Wicks (1854–1919) were educated at Cornell, opened an office in Auburn, N.Y. in 1880, and moved to Buffalo between 1884 and 1886. Together until 1917, they designed the Albright Gallery, the YMCA, the Chamber of Commerce building, the Buffalo Savings Bank and 16 buildings of the university.

81. William E. Spier residence, Glens Falls, N.Y.; Robert W. Gibson, architect, n.d. Gibson (1854–1927) was unusual among these architects because he was not an American by birth. Born in Aveley, Essex, he won silver medals for architectural drawing in 1877 and 1878 while studying at the Royal Academy of Arts, and then traveled through Europe prior to emigrating to the United States in 1881. Settling in Albany in partnership with William Pretyman, he won the competition for All Saints, the Episcopal Cathedral of Albany. He moved to New York City in 1888 where he remained a popular architect of revival styles and served two terms as president of the New York Architectural League. Gibson's decision to practice in the United States was probably a difficult one to make. British architects and critics in the early 1880s regarded Yankeeland as the home of architectural "humbug," where "licking all creation" was valued above sound, knowledgeable design. Furthermore, designing an American suburban house that looked indigenous was a challenging assignment for a British-trained architect. Comparatively speaking, English houses in similar settings probably would have looked more formal and substantial and would have been less active spatially and less varied in texture and materials. Nevertheless, Gibson produced an American-looking house of the 1880s. The round arches and heavy stone work were popular in these years as were the contrast of round and square-cut shingles, the curving wall of the drawing room and the combination of gables of different sizes. The exterior was appropriately animated and sufficiently varied in surface and color. There were also features that seemed somewhat unusual, though these could be attributed to Gibson's distinctive style or his weakness as a designer as well as to his possible failure to comprehend American domestic work or his desire to continue to draw upon British practices. For example, the arcade of the loggia was quite monastic, the course separating the first and second floors an atypical transition of the mid-1880s, the rounded porch excessively high and the main porch restrained for a principal veranda. In fact, the plan indicates that a more ex-

pressive piazza was contemplated. Finally, the large number of separate spaces of the main floor was unusual and, in this specific case, is a reflection of the functional compartmentalization of the English Victorian house. A commercial building occupies this site on Glen Street today. The obituary notice for Spier (1849–1901) claimed that "Glens Falls has suffered a loss which none can fully appreciate." A partner in the Morgan Lumber Co. in 1873, he organized the Glens Falls Collar Company in 1876, the first of many shirt-making concerns in the city, and the Glens Falls Paper Mill Co. in 1885, and was one of the creators of the International Paper Co. in 1898. He used this house as a summer home after 1888, when he moved his principal residence to New York City.

82. Cordelia Sterling residence, Stratford, Conn.; Bruce Price and Rufus W. Bunnell, architects, 1886. Pleased with the quality of house design in the United States, Price wrote in 1893, "In the building of the moderate-cost suburban villa of today, the American architect has no equal. I believe his work is well above and beyond any period of the school anywhere. Of course, I mean his best work. There is much that is bad, very bad; there have been many conditions to make it so. Vulgar and ambitious clients, uncultivated draughtsmen, who, gifted with clever manual dexterity (and our draughtsmen are getting to be very, very clever as such), set up as architects; *nouveaux riches*, who gauge the beauty of their house by its cost; these and many other conditions produce inevitably their results. But when the client and his architect are in accord . . . the results are noble and true." This was one commission, however, in which his relationship with his client was probably not ideal. John W. Sterling, descendant of a family that arrived in New England in 1651, commissioned the house for his mother and two sisters, Cordelia and Catharine, but the finished product may owe more to Rufus W. Bunnell than Price intended. Bunnell was a builder in Stratford who married Catharine. Assuming responsibility for the construction, Bunnell evidently attempted to show Price how the project could be improved. The two argued; Sheldon attributed the final work to both men. Price's hand may be detected in several exterior elements that also appeared in the Baker house (plate 19): the brickwork, flat-arch window heads, sections of rectangular voids, octagonal tower, high triple window, shape of the chimney, knobs of the roof and unfluted columns with entasis. The handling of the roofs in both houses was quite similar. The eclecticism of this exterior does suggest Price, but the hardness and awkwardness of the design are less convincing. The relationship between the measured but stiff portico and the main body of the structure is particularly weak. The floor plan is similarly uninspired. Six relatively small rooms are arranged in two rows neatly but without much imagi-

nation, an interior that reflects little of the flair and confidence Price had demonstrated in the plan of the Neff house (plate 71) at Cincinnati four years earlier. However, these rooms were expensively finished; oak was used for the wainscoting and paneling of the hall, cherry for the wainscoting of the dining room and the library, and natural whitewood with gold leaf trim in the parlor. Given to Stratford through Cordelia's will, the house at 2283 Main Street has served since 1932 as the Sterling House Community Center.

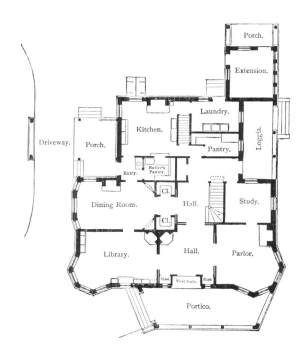

83. John H. Cheever residence, Far Rockaway, N.Y.; McKim, Mead & White, architects, 1886. As the decade progressed this firm designed halls that became increasingly larger, geometrically simpler and more self-contained. This appealed to Sheldon, who never tired of pointing out that the great-manor house halls of fifteenth-century England would be a noble prototype for contemporary American designers to adapt for modern use. The imaginative interpenetration of space that had characterized American planning in the early 1880s was not present in this arrangement. Instead, the major rooms were relatively independent spaces, linked together but without intimacy. In centrifugal planning—from the inside outward—the interior influenced the exterior; here the interior was a consequence of the semi-octagonal perimeter. Though the relationship between the major rooms was not organic, the architects incorporated functional elements cleverly. The placement of the fireplace in the hall balanced focal points on the three remaining sides. In the wedge to the right of the parlor entrance they included a recess with curved shelves. The driveway facade conveyed the impression of orderliness, controlled ingenuity and formal generosity. The firm labored to relieve the mirror-image effect. Windows on one side were not matched on the other, the central chimney was off center and the enclosed laundry-kitchen area was answered by superimposed porches. But these porches became visually isolated from the rest of the house. The ionic entrance was unusually learned for the unpretentious brick and shingled wall behind it and, especially, for the eye windows of the roof. Furthermore, the architects may have missed an opportunity to restate at this entrance the quiet assurance of the low and simple hip roofs on either wing. Nevertheless, this was a significant house in this series and a cleaner statement of several of the ideas that McKim, Mead & White ex-

pressed in their Appleton house (plate 15). Its plan and elevation represented a critique of spatial informality and picturesque massing by an influential firm concerned about the maturing of American architecture. By comparison, the exuberance of the Queen Anne, though delightful and refreshing, may have seemed naïve. The house was also prophetic, in its horizontal sweep and high windows darkened by the projecting roof, of Frank Lloyd Wright's work in the early twentieth century. Although the house has often been identified as "Wave Crest," this designation refers to a section of Far Rockaway originally created as a private park with an entrance and more than a dozen houses within. Cheever, who died in 1901 at the age of 77, was one of the oldest residents of the park. He was president of the New York Belting and Packing Co. and the Mechanical Rubber Co. This $17,000 house was demolished in the 1940s.

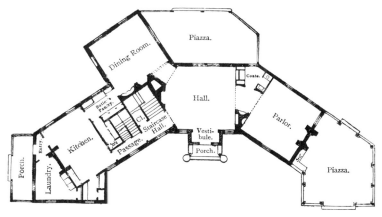

84. Thomas T. Kinney residence, Elberon, N.J.; Van Campen Taylor, architect, 1882. In the mid-1880s thousands of summer guests stayed for various lengths of time on the Long Branch coast. They could travel from New York in 2¼ hours for $1 and from Philadelphia in 3½ hours for $2. President Grant made frequent visits to this area during his term in office, 1869–77, making it in effect the summer capital of the country. Presidents Hayes and Harrison stayed at the Elberon Hotel and President James Garfield asked to be taken to Elberon to die after being shot in Washington in the summer of 1881. He was gently transported to the Francklyn Cottage, designed by McKim, Mead & White, which was located near their Newcomb house (plate 76) and across Ocean Avenue from the future site of their Cook house (plate 14). The Kinney cottage, near the Cook site, was probably completed in the year following Garfield's death. Its owner, born in Newark in 1827, took a law degree at Princeton but never practiced because he succeeded his father as editor of the Newark *Daily Advertiser* in 1851 and managed the paper until he retired in 1892. Sheldon probably thought highly of this house because it contained enough evidence of the contemporary movement to look up-to-date and at the same time featured enough forms and ornament from the past to satisfy his appetite for educated eclecticism. While the horizontality of the clapboard and shingle layers and the arrangement of windows in series were contemporary touches, Taylor also complicated his facade with carefully placed effects that may look contrived, applied or isolated: the turned posts of the porte cochere, the circular motif under the gable, the eyelid dormer, the blunt oriel and the ribbed-and-banded chimneys. This facade suggests a designer who repeatedly stood back from his basic composition to see where he could add one more piece of architectural interest. Certainly, Taylor could have added more than he did, but he also could have tied his effects to a clearer program. His

plan, however, was relatively straightforward, and the major spaces were wide, airy and light. The hall was darker than surrounding rooms because its access to light was limited and because the redwood beams of its ceiling were two feet lower than the ceilings of adjacent spaces. Somewhat unusual was Taylor's treatment of the entrance hall as a pleasant and well-lighted sitting room while the hall itself served primarily as a showpiece and traffic concourse. Built on a brick foundation (55′ × 110′), with clapboards to the floor of the second story and pine shingles on the upper walls and roof, the house cost $15,000. It has been demolished. The architect is not well-known. He was born in the 1840s in New Brunswick, N.J., practiced in Newark and later moved his office to New York City. He died in 1906.

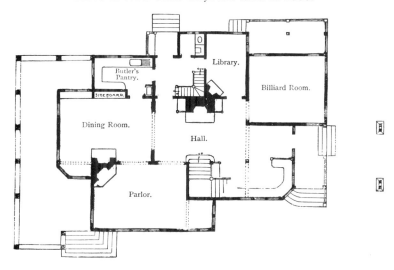

85. "Clifton," James Elverson residence, Washington, D.C.; Addison Hutton, architect, 1885. Elverson, who lived in Philadelphia, chose this site at 3401 Whitehaven Street, N.W., for his "country seat." Born in England in 1838, he came to the United States when 11, learned to operate the telegraph and managed the Washington office of telegraphic communications during the Civil War. After the war he turned to journalism, publishing *The Saturday Night*, and in 1880 he founded the widely read children's magazine *Golden Days*. In 1889 he acquired the Philadelphia *Inquirer*. He died in 1911. The walls of this house were of rock-faced Potomac bluestone, the roof of slate, the sills, courses, and copings of brownstone; the sparse amount of wood used on the exterior was painted a dull red. The old mansion was destroyed by fire in November, 1949. The design was an attempt to join together dissimilar and even contradictory statements. If the crenelation of the tower provoked visions of archers quickly turning an advance into a rout, the wraparound, all-American veranda implied that the door was open all the time. If the corbie or crowstep gables celebrated the European past, the shingles of the tower and the wooden piazza reaffirmed the American present. Sheldon offered an explanation. "During his travels in Europe, Mr. Elverson's attention was often attracted to the effects of broken skylines, and, when determining to build a house for himself, he resolved to reproduce in it some of the most interesting of those results. At the same time, as Washington is a southern city, he could not ignore the natural fitness of the veranda or gallery." The veranda, which appears to undulate as well as to move forward and backward, prepared visitors for a much less tightly planned interior than they discovered. Judging from the large vestibule, the carefully placed and shaped reception room, the spaciousness

of both parlor and dining room and the banishment of the kitchen's noise and smells from this level, Elverson must have intended to entertain and to entertain quite formally. Though somewhat didactic, this arrangement was socially efficient, for its labyrinth led guests systematically from the entrance to the reception room to talk, then to dinner and then to the after-dinner separation of the sexes in the library and the parlor. The tone of the hall and dining room was conditioned largely by the dark oak woodwork, the mirrors of plate glass and the windows of stained glass. Hardwoods were used, except in the parlor, which was painted an ivory white.

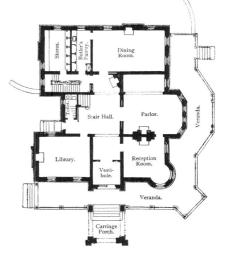

86. "Sunset Cottage," Alonzo B. Rich residence, Short Hills, N.J.; Lamb and Rich, architects, 1882. Then in the first year of his partnership with Hugo Lamb, Charles Rich undoubtedly designed this house commissioned by his parents, the Rev. and Mrs. Alonzo B. Rich. In fact, he probably lived here himself prior to his marriage to Harriet R. Bradbury, also a resident of Short Hills. On the third floor was his studio, its exposed ceiling beams and weathered brick fireplace suggesting a masculine environment and its billiard table, telescope and telegraphic apparatus revealing his hobbies. Under the roof of the oriel the younger Rich created a darkroom for his amateur photography. The original arrangement of the house called for four bedrooms on the second floor but only two major family spaces on the first. There was no vestibule to announce the hall; visitors entered the "inner-sanctum" immediately. Because the hall was too small for a sitting room and too exposed to the exterior to be comfortable, it served primarily as a traffic artery, but one which, given stature by the main stairway, quickly lost its social importance where it abruptly became a back hallway. The nearness of the back stairway to the main stairs was peculiar. While the dining room and parlor were spacious areas and could be linked together easily, they were not shaped by an abundance of imagination. Perhaps the earnestly plastic octagon was a conscious effort to compensate for such matter-of-fact planning. Miraculously, this dry plan blossomed into an exterior that looks warm and lively without appearing to be contrived. Conservative within, Rich gambled in designing the outside. He wrote its name, "Sunset Cottage," in beach pebbles on the panel above the window of the hall and a Latin inscription, "Ars longa est, vita brevis est" (Art is long; life is short), on a sundial of the parlor wall. Contemporaries sometimes hooted at his veritable sunset of colors, graded from gray-yellow stained shingles under the gable to dark red at the base, a transition from light to dark that is visible in the photograph. He employed a variety of material—rough stone, brick and wood used as shingles, clapboards and board and batten—to heighten the picturesqueness of the surface. The architect fashioned from a rigid plan an exterior that appears to have difficulty containing the expanding volumes within. This impression is conveyed specifically through the oriel, its bell roof, the gambrel roof above the rear porch and the entasis of the chimney. The house is still occupied at 12 The Cresent, but this facade has been slightly altered.

87. "Stoneacre," John W. Ellis residence, Newport, R.I.; William A. Potter, architect, 1882–85. If size were the measure of excellence, then the Ellis house could qualify as the Parthenon of *Artistic Country-Seats*. With terrace, its dimension were 118′ × 100′. It contained seven chimneys, 18 bedrooms and a main hall, exclusive of the stairway hall, which occupied about 625 square feet. Potter tried to control and discipline this behemoth by flanking it with a veranda composed of powerful arched bays. Similarly, he marked off the progress of the house at roof level through the phalanx of oversize dormers. Thus, above and below he selected a substantial basic unit and, repeating it without variation, developed a decisive cadence along the major facade of the house. Sensing that the result, though firm, could also be interpreted as too hard and too rigid, Potter may have introduced the circular and semi-octagonal projections of the near side to soften the general impression. One can probably judge the size of the house more accurately by focusing on the long flank of the piazza than by examining the plan. Actually, the drawing room was 27′ × 18′ and the dining room 40′ long. In addition to the five guest and three servant bedrooms on the third floor, there was also a male preserve consisting of a smoking room (23′ × 20′) and a billiard room (32′ × 28′). Morning rooms and boudoirs were not common in these houses. The boudoir could be part of a bedroom suite or, as in this case, a modest sitting room used by the mistress of the house. Edith Wharton once described the morning room as "a kind of undress drawing room where the family may gather informally at all hours of the day." She recommended furnishings that were "plain, comfortable, and capable of resisting hard use." Despite its sheer volume and debts to English country-house planning, and despite the growing popularity for natural hardwoods in this period, most of the interior of the Ellis house was finished in pine which was painted, except in the dining room where the wood was stained because of the room's importance. In keeping with the practice of the day, Potter de-emphasized the visibility of the servants' wing. The projecting bay of the dining room and

the bedroom block and smoking room above it discouraged curiosity beyond this point. The two dormers and chimney of the rear section repeated forms on the public side but were reduced in size and placed at a lower level. The house, which faced Bellevue Avenue, has been razed. Ellis (b. 1817) established the 1st National Bank in Cincinnati and in 1869 moved to New York to manage the Bank of Winslow, Lanier and Company. After the failure of the Northern Pacific Railroad in 1873, he helped to revive the line and remained one of its directors until 1886. Potter (1842–1909) son of the well-known Alonzo Potter, Episcopal Bishop of Pennsylvania, was highly influenced by the work of Richardson. Recent publications by Sarah B. Landau and Lawrence Wodehouse have added much to our previously limited understanding of Potter.

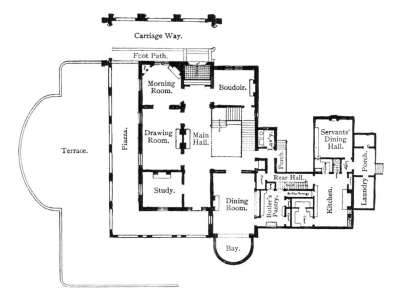

88. "Cliffs," George D. Howe residence, Manchester-by-the-Sea, Mass.; Arthur Little, architect, 1879. Arthur Little (1852–1925) studied architecture at M.I.T. between 1871 and 1876, worked briefly for the firm of Peabody and Stearns, and opened his own office in Boston in 1879. As Walter Sturgis noted, the Howe house of that year was an unexpected commission. The clients were well-connected Bostonians who had inherited the fortune Howe's father had made in real estate. Little, on the other hand, had never built a house and, evidently, had never finished his architectural studies. "Cliffs" was an early manifestation of the growing appreciation for the clapboarded houses of eighteenth-century America, a trend inspired partially by three exhibition buildings at the Philadelphia Centennial and encouraged by the admiration of such architects as Emerson, McKim and Peabody for Colonial work. Little made an important contribution to the movement when he published in the winter of 1877–78 *Early New England Interiors*, 36 informative but dry sketches intended to "preserve the relics of a style fast disappearing." In his one-page preface, he recommended the revival of this style "which is everywhere marked with peculiar dignity, simplicity, and refinement." The Howe house is characterized by these three qualities. It also contains several specific features found in Georgian Colonial houses: the light color, basically symmetrical organization of facade and rectangular perimeter of the main section, hipped roof with evenly spaced dormers and roof balustrade, two-story corner pilasters, a modest, classical cornice below the eaves, fan windows and the centrally placed hall with two rooms to either side. The house also contained features not characteristic of eighteenth-century work: the angled plan, shingles instead of clapboards, projections of the den and parlor alcove, location of the chimneys, the Japanese-inspired wooden screens and, most obviously, the enveloping veranda which links the house intimately with the site. Little cleverly deemphasized the servants' wing by lowering its

roof and eliminating both dormers and balustrade. He made its facade less forthright by covering it with trellis and ivy and discouraged curiosity by raising the window level. Also, the den's prominent rectangle states that what lies beyond it is not consequential. Inside, the hall walls were covered with Chinese paper in bright colors against a white ground, those of the parlor were finished in blue-and-white paper and the library was pine painted a golden yellow with a red and white dado of straw matting. Built for approximately $15,000, "Cliffs" remains relatively unchanged on Smith's Point. Although Scully dated it ca. 1886 on stylistic grounds, Sturgis, citing tax records, claimed it was completed in 1879.

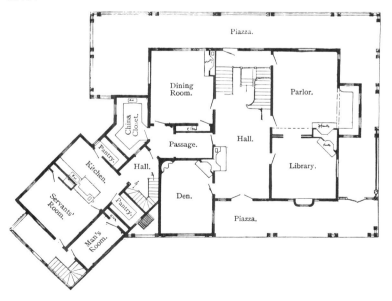

89. "Grasshead," James L. Little residence, Swampscott, Mass.; Arthur Little, architect, 1882. The house that Little designed for his parents at Swampscott was not as dignified, simple and refined as the Howe house (plate 88) of 1879. Built for $12,000 and still extant, though radically transformed, "Grasshead" was more playful and loosely composed. The second story in shingles held the 120′-long facade together but not dogmatically so. Against this continuous dark band, Little set idiosyncratic, plastic forms: an abruptly terminated octagonal tower, a bulbous entrance hood too ponderous for the wall that supports it and a lighthouse isolated from the body of the house by the rectangular void of the breezeway. Little seemed to suggest that these "pop" elements be enjoyed independently of the rest of the elevation, but because he covered them with shingles also, we cannot disengage them from the whole. The playfulness of this facade reflected the self-confidence of both client and architect. The untrimmed tree trunks of the piazza were among the most antihistorical and professionally risky elements in the entire series. In January of 1887 the most influential British architectural journal, *The Builder*, objected to Little's bucolic experiment. Explaining that previously there had been a paucity of originality in American architecture but today too much, the journal charged that similar untrimmed poles, which Little had employed on a house at Lobster Cove, Manchester-by-the-Sea, Mass., represented "an absurd affectation of rusticity which is at variance with architectural principles and good taste." At the entrance the purity and refinement of the small round windows, by contrast, made the beehive canopy appear even heavier. To the left of the vestibule was a small music room, atypically relegated to the servants' side of the house. To the right

was the hall (28′ × 14′), decorated with a 5′ dado of pine, blue-and-red Chinese paper of fish in the sea, and a ceiling of dark-stained beams. There were also distinctive features in the parlor—the white half-staircase leading to the landing of the main staircase and the deeply recessed fireplace flanked by identical quarter-circle windows and cane-backed settees. This inglenook suggested a hallowed space for ritualistic family councils. In the lighthouse above the smoking room, which also served as a changing room for bathers, was a lookout reached by outside walkways. On the second floor, the most unusual room was the "tent-room," a spacious bedroom (20′ × 15′ × 18′) in which the walls sloped in every direction from a midpoint in the ceiling. Its manner so suited to the life of the seaside, "Grasshead" is a remarkable example of the architecture of relaxation. It enriched the grand tradition of architecture by not taking its authority too seriously. In 1833 James Lovell Little (1810–1889) formed the dry-goods firm of Little, Alden & Co., which 20 years later became James L. Little & Co. He was one of the incorporators of M.I.T. and one of the founders of the Union Club of Boston.

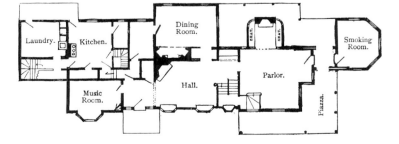

90. William F. Weld residence, Brookline, Mass.; Edmund M. Wheelwright, architect, 1887. Sheldon stressed the fine decoration of the main floor of the Weld house. "The spirit of the interior decoration is that of the early Italian Renaissance, which appears in the smallest details of the hall and oaken staircase, and pervades, with less strictness of purpose, all the other rooms. The Caen stone of the hall mantel is enlivened with color and with gold; and Mr. Francis Lathrop has designed the ornamentation for the wall spaces, covering them with canvas painted in arabesques and strap-work, to the height of the caps of the columns and the pilasters. The staircase, from first story to attic, is hung with tapestries. In the drawing-room, the finish is in pine, painted an enamel white, and touched up with gold. The shutter-boxes extend into the room, and are decorated with delicately carved and fluted Doric columns and pilasters. The low wooden dado has a small perpendicular paneling, and the carved frieze shows garlands and fruit. The walls are covered with light-blue silk, and the plaster garlands of the ceiling entwine themselves in low relief about figures painted by Mr. Francis Lathrop. The dimensions of this room are eighteen feet by twenty-one. Somewhat larger is the mahogany dining-room—eighteen feet by twenty-nine and a half—its walls covered with red tapestry, and its sideboard occupying the entire side opposite the windows. Heavy beams divide the ceiling into three parts, and frame some decorative panels designed by the Tiffany Glass Company. The walls of the billiard-room—twenty feet by twenty-two and a half—show leather, studded with brass nails." Wheelwright's somewhat unorthodox plan was functional and engaging. Arranged logically within the servants' wing, its rooms also connected easily with the dining room, main hall and outside stairs. Both the dining room and the drawing room were reasonably well isolated from the noise and tobacco odors of the billiard room. The intimacy of the hall bay was a

natural preface for the corner study. Flexibly related to the bay and the drawing room, the hall could be seen as a simple small area or a complicated, larger one. The elevation appeared lower than it was because Wheelwright stressed horizontal movements—the shingles that looked like clapboarding, the strips of trim and the long, narrow Roman brick. Furthermore, he announced this horizontality by creating a vast plateau walled by rock-face granite. The site, off Newton Street, is today known as Anderson Park; the house has been destroyed. "One of Boston's wealthiest citizens," according to a newspaper obituary, Weld (1855–1893) paid $90,000 for his house and $40,000 for his stable, which is still standing. Erected about 1889, he dedicated it with one of the costliest barn parties in Boston's social history.

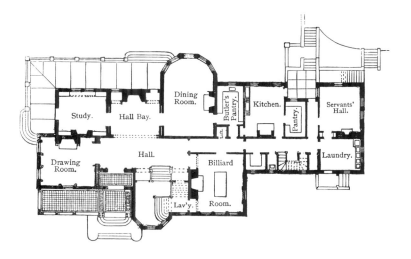

91. "Naumkeag," Joseph H. Choate residence, Stockbridge, Mass.; McKim, Mead & White, architects, 1886–87. The term eclectic, meaning selected from diverse sources, is often used pejoratively in reference to architecture. However, in the fruitful 1880s eclecticism flourished in American domestic work. The summer home of the Choates in the Berkshire Hills, not one of McKim, Mead & White's finest but certainly representative of a type of country seat in this period, was unabashedly eclectic. The porch, looking like a section stolen from a Greek stoa, was carried out with unexpected attention to detail. Because of its sophistication, erudition and formality, it becomes a Mediterranean intruder into the manorial memories stirred up by the approach side. Here we are invited to imagine that these irregular, lichen-covered stones have been retrieved from old English ruins to serve modern gentry. The architects utilized the American shingled roof as the agent to hold these vestiges of the Greeks and the English together. This penchant of both architects and clients in a period of unprecedented domestic technology for materials and elements that were crude or archaic is intriguing. Was such country architecture asked to embody customs and memories threatened by urban and industrial growth? "Naumkeag" was built for approximately $46,000 by Choate (1832–1917), who had summered in this area since 1874, before it became fashionable for New Yorkers to spend some time in the Berkshires after the Newport season had ended and before the city winter season had begun. One of the nation's best-known and wittiest lawyers, he fought the constitutionality of the graduated income tax before the Supreme Court in 1895, convincing the justices to reverse their position. He was ambassador to Britain from 1899 to 1905. The house has not been fully completed; note the workmen, horse and cart and materials at the far right. The arrangement in which the hall, as a sitting room, occupied the bar in the H-shape of the plan was common in the work of this firm in the mid-1880s. By shifting the study and service rooms to the extreme right, the magnificent view of the valley was not obstructed. A planned schoolroom was unusual in these large summer houses. Even rarer was a specific space in which the kerosene lamps, which replaced whale-oil lamps in the early 1860s, were filled and cleaned. White's decorative skill was evident within. Of the parlor, Sheldon wrote, "The delicately worked members of its high base; the finely molded and carved architraves of its doors and windows; and the elaborate frieze and cornice—the frieze with a treatment of ribbons and a light ball-ornament—all attract the refined and sensitive taste." "Naumkeag" is extant.

92. "Netherfield," Elizabeth Kidder residence, Beverly Farms, Mass.; Sturgis and Brigham, architects, 1886. In 1865 Henry Kidder (1823–1886) became principal partner of Kidder, Peabody and Co., which subsequently became the leading banking house of New England. In 1883 he married his second wife, Elizabeth Huidekoper of Meadville, Pa., and this coastal home at Beverly Farms was a by-product of the marriage. Kidder died in January, 1886, before the work was completed, but stipulated in his will that the unfinished house belonged to Mrs. Kidder, who also received their town house in Boston while the family estate at Milton, Mass. went to one of his sons. The cost of this weekend and summer cottage was approximately $100,000. Long and narrow, 143' by an average of 40', it was divided into two parts held together on the main floor by a corridor and the butler's entrance to the dining room. This separation was maintained on the second floor where, above the work area, there were eight bedrooms for servants. The plan of the family space was much simpler and less frenetic than the exterior implied. Three huge rooms, the sitting room-hall (21' × 41'), the dining room (a dodecagon 24' in diameter) and the parlor (18' × 28'), expanded toward the ocean, which could be seen best from the 8'-square pane of glass in the bay window of the hall and from the 10'-wide bay of the parlor. Screened by the prominent stairway of the hall, the corridor enabled servants to reach the front porch without disturbing family or guests. Native gray field granite was used for the ground and first levels and weathered shingles with dark green trim for the superstructure. Stylistically, the house was unique but not easily categorized. Its stone base was Romanesque in mood but less so in detail while above the surfaces were shingled and the skyline animated by Queen Anne forms. Despite Sheldon's frequent references to the necessity of truth and simple beauty, he selected numerous residences for inclusion in *Artistic Country-Seats*

which, to the contrary, were complicated and often ostentatious. The Kidder house was a good example. Ignoring its overtaxed composition and ponderous scale, he defended it as "a building skillfully adapted to its surroundings, designed in all its details and embellishments in accordance with true artistic feeling, and having an expression of harmony with the purpose for which it was constructed." Demolished in 1966, this house was located on a private road off Paine Avenue, near Pride's Crossing in Beverly Farms. A portion of it was incorporated into a remodeled building on the site. Sturgis (1834–1888) and Brigham (d. 1925) formed a Boston firm best known for the city's older Museum of Fine Arts, which was completed in 1876. John Sturgis left the partnership in 1886 and a year later returned to England, where he had spent much of his youth.

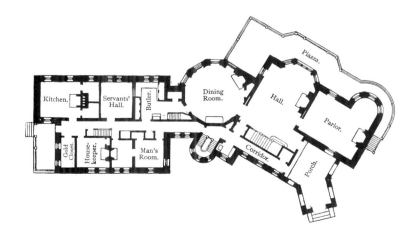

93. Spencer Trask residence, Saratoga Springs, N.Y.; A. Page Brown, architect, 1886. Both the elevation and the plan of the Trask house were unusual. Disregarding the relative tranquility of the lower stories, the tower, overscaled but providing marvelous views of the 600 acres owned by the Trask family, enlivened the roof and became the focal point of the composition. Laterally, the first floor was divided into distinct sections: from left to right, a shingled wall, the glass of the dining room, a section of unidentified material set in undulating layers and the veranda outlined with columns. The sweeping curves of the terrace and the veranda defined space expansively while the box-shaped family section of the plan, by comparison, appeared to be shaped by a foreordained geometric perimeter. Normally, the central hall would have continued through the left end of the library, providing access to the servants' quarters, instead of depending on the dining room for this purpose. We could explain the reasons for these distinctive features if the history of the house were less complicated. Though identified by Sheldon as a structure of 1886 designed by Brown, a section, possibly the servants' wing, was built in the 1850s and owned by a Dr. Childs. Trask purchased this house on Union Avenue, east of the racetrack, in 1881 and had it remodeled twice, once, probably in the early 1880s, by S. Gifford Slocum of Saratoga Springs, and the second time probably by A. Page Brown in 1885 or 1886. The second alteration, photographed here, cost approximately $75,000, much of which was spent on interior decoration: the hall (23′ × 21′) had a paneled ceiling but no wainscot; the drawing room (17′ × 23′) contained a mantel supported by columns of Mexican onyx and a French beveled mirror, while its walls were covered with silk tapestries; the library (24′ × 14′) had shelves of oak and walls embellished with stamped leather; the dining room (24′ × 16′) was done in stained cherry. Most of the 15 bedrooms were covered with wallpapers by William Morris, and each of the eight bedrooms on the second floor contained a fireplace of Roman brick. This house burned in 1891. Two years later W. Halsey Wood designed for the site a new house, "Yaddo," which since 1926 has been a retreat for writers, composers and artists. Trask (1844–1909) was born in New York City. completed his studies at Princeton in 1866 and became a successful Wall Street banker, a director of several railroads and president of the Edison Electric Illuminating Company. After his education at Cornell, Brown (1859–1896) worked for McKim, Mead & White for three years before he established his own practice in 1885 in New York. Four years later he moved to San Francisco where, until his accidental death, he was one of California's more influential architects.

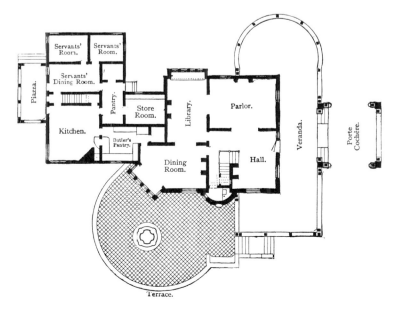

94. "Elm Court," William D. Sloane residence, Lenox, Mass.; Peabody and Stearns, architects, 1886–87. Sloane became treasurer of the well-known W. and J. Sloane Co., a carpet and upholstery firm that his father had established in New York City. When this structure was finished, it was one of the largest frame houses Peabody and Stearns had executed, and Sheldon remarked that "most visitors at Lenox, Mass. consider Mr. William D. Sloane's magnificent new villa the most important architectural attraction of the place." The "architectural attraction" of the house eludes easy description because it is so large and because it looks as if it had been put together additively. Its scale can be sensed from the dimensions of the major rooms: the main hall, 35′ × 22′; the library, 22′ × 20′; the dining room, 38′ × 28′; and the guest chamber, 28′ × 18′. Although the cohesiveness of the house was strengthened by the pervasive shingles, the repetition of the gable form, the echo of the roof lines and chimneys following a basic form and finish, the house rambles across the landscape as if it were consciously mocking those "responsible" architectural strictures about unity, clarity, focus. Its mission appears to be the consumption of maximum acreage with minimum inhibition. In order to pour new wealth into old wineskins, Peabody and Stearns intentionally left the impression that additions had been built to the central section over the years. Their motives aside, the architects and client were not afraid to try the unexpected or the unconventional. They placed a shingled house on a white marble foundation, a peculiar combination perhaps, but evidently justified because the marble was obtained locally and was cheaper than any other suitable material. Although the library was finished in cherry with walls of leather, the great hall—"a more comfortable sitting-room than this spacious hall does not exist on this side of the Atlantic," claimed Sheldon—was done in pine, and painted pine at that. Sloane's "own room," detached from the rest of the house, was unique in the houses included in *Artistic Country-Seats*. Also, the location of the guest chamber on the main floor overlooking the driveway was certainly atypical of planning practices of the day. Because summer residents at Lenox spent much of their time traveling from one house to another by carriage,

buggy or horseback, the driveway became an essential part of the grounds. The parade of carriages traditionally occurred every afternoon in the main street of the village. Sloane kept more than 20 driving and saddle horses in his stables and maintained a staff of six grooms to care for them and the equipment. The horses grazed on 100 acres that cost him $50,000. Though altered (see photographs in *American Architect and Building News*, Apr. 5, 1902) and now unoccupied, the house remains on the Old Stockbridge Road three miles from Lenox.

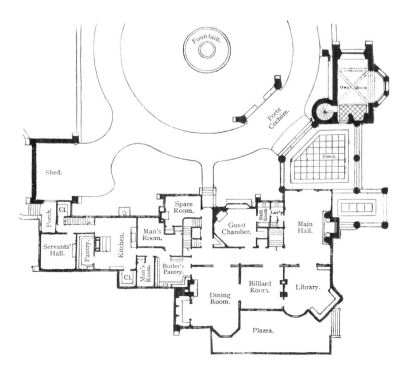

95. "Beaurivage," John B. Dyar residence, Grosse Pointe Farms, Mich.; Mason and Rice, architects, 1886. Designer of many of Detroit's noted structures, among them the old and new Masonic Temples, the Opera House, the Yacht Club, Hotel Pontchartrain and the Standard Savings and Loan Building, Mason (1856–1948) was described in obituaries as the dean of Michigan architects. After a high-school education and apprenticeships with two local firms, he began his partnership with Zacharias Rice in 1878. In his fine study of Detroit's architecture, W. Hawkins Ferry reported that Mason predicted the decline of wood in American work after an 1884 tour of Europe during which he discovered that the material was used much more sparingly than in the United States. Though he did employ harder materials increasingly, the Dyar house, finished two years after this European trip, demonstrated why wood remained the preferred material for domestic architecture during the 1880s. It was cheap; this house facing Lake St. Clair cost $8,500. The smooth pine clapboards of the first floor and the California redwood shingles of the veranda, second floor and gables illustrated its varied manifestations. Mason chose shades of dark olive for the walls and dark red for the shingles, proving its chromatic advantages. Easily shaped, wood could be used for the broad arches of the veranda or the intricately turned spindles. Mason was not entirely comfortable with the shingle surface, controlling it through emphatic layers and hiding it in key places. Nevertheless, he produced for the Dyars an attractive house in a style we normally associate with New England, New York and New Jersey. Though peculiar in shape, the plan was quite contemporary, and recognized through the spacious servants' section the increasing bargaining power of domestic help in the 1880s. The two kitchens plus supporting rooms were approximately equal in size to the space used by the family. Mason's plan illustrated the pivotal role given the hall by many architects in these years. The heart of the vertical and horizontal activity of its inhabitants, the hall, in black ash, was also the primary space for receiving and entertaining. The dining room, of quartered white oak, and the bay, a cross between a parlor and an alcove, though devoid of the common fireplace, were really extensions of this vital area. Dyar (1846–1898) founded a series of companies that produced radiators for steam and hot-water systems. He was also responsible for the interurban railroad line between Detroit and Port Huron, built in the 1890s. "Ever ready to aid in all social pleasures," according to a local author in 1886, Dyar frequently entertained the leaders of Detroit's pre-car society at "Beaurivage." Built at 65 Lakeshore Drive at the corner of Sunset Lane, the house was demolished in February, 1942.

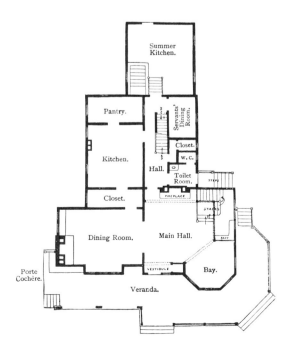

96. "Brownleigh Hall," James Wentworth Brown residence, Needham, Mass.; Allen and Kenway, architects, 1883. The Brown house was distinctive in several respects. The plan looked as though the architects had shaped individual rooms and then pushed them together to form an interior. Both the billiard and morning rooms were indebted to those in English nineteenth-century country estates. Cotton's *Compleat Gamster* (1674) was the first English book to include billiards, this "gentile, cleanly, and most ingenious game" played on "something longer than it is broad" and "rail'd round, which rail ought to be a little swel'd or stuft with fine flox/wool/or cotton." Though they became the principal men's retreat in English country houses, rooms exclusively used for billiards did not appear until the early nineteenth century. The large, symmetrically shaped hall was based on the great halls of late medieval England. Two stories high and brightly illuminated by banks of windows on the west and east, its main features were the wide fireplace on the north and the stairway-balcony complex opposite it. Despite the evidence of piecemeal planning, the architects preserved long but narrow perspectives, from the vestibule into the morning room and from the dining room to the hearth of the hall. On the other hand, the angled plan, more confidently stated by Emerson, Little, Peabody and Stearns, and McKim, Mead & White, was a sign of experimentation in these years and the leg of the L was one of the most efficient means of joining the servants' quarters to the core of the house. A mixture of derivative and contemporary tendencies was also evident on the exterior. To the main block of early English half-timbering, its solidity compromised by many square feet of glass, the architects appended an impermanent-looking American veranda of wood. Curiously, they squeezed a balcony between the chimney and the hall, interrupting the coolness of the paneled facade. The recessed entrance to the morning room contained an excellent example of the extent to which doors could be treated simultaneously as windows. The harmonious color scheme ranged from the Indian red of the roof, through the reddish brown of the timber, to the lighter panels and pink granite. Built at the corner of Grove Street and Charles River Street on land once part of the remarkable 800-acre park developed by William Emerson Baker, the house was totally destroyed by fire in April, 1926. Brown, who died in 1894 at the age of 67, was a merchant associated with Lewis, Brown & Co. of Boston. The valuation of the land in 1883 was $4,000, of the house $28,500 and of the barn $2,500. At the time of its destruction the house was valued at $125,000. Francis R. Allen (1843–1931) and Arthur Kenway became partners in Boston after Allen returned from study in Paris in 1879; the relationship lasted until 1890. Allen designed eight buildings for Williams College and 12 for Vassar.

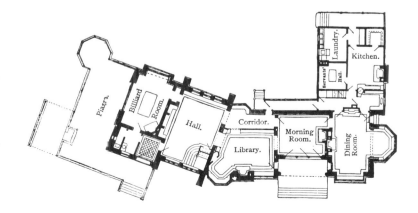

97. J. Randolph Coolidge residence, Brookline, Mass.; C. Howard Walker, architect, 1885–86. Before it was removed, this stone-and-shingle structure stretched across a knoll, the crown of a 25-acre property on Heath Street near the Chestnut Hill reservoir in Brookline. When this photograph was taken, Coolidge (1828–1925), a lawyer, and his family had probably not moved in or were in the process of moving in, judging from the absence of porch furniture, curtains, interior decoration or activity, and the evidence that not much attention had, as yet, been given to the grounds. Because it does not reveal those signs of human imprint which are so easily taken for granted and because there were no trees to take the edge off its newness, the house looked more naked and less melodic than Walker probably would have wished. Nevertheless, it illustrates well many of the basic traits of American domestic work in the 1880s—the combination of varied and often unrefined materials, the search for texture and color harmonies that would blend with the natural setting, the convention of combining a firm base with an animated superstructure, building from the inside outward, the belief that American space was limitless, the belief that human beings should dwell horizontally. This was expressive architecture requiring of its designers imagination and spirit. They risked new recipes for their banquets. Walker's meal was not entirely satisfactory. Built from stone taken from old walls in the neighborhood, the base was meant to express age and stability, but its corollary message of crudity was too strong because Walker carried the wall too high and increased the impression of rawness by contrasting it with Medford granite. The granite of the porch piers and the trim under the dining-room windows were used to distinguish between the royal and working sections of the house. This transition from prized to primitive materials was also noticeable in the relationship between the level of the first floor and the slanting ground; the family piazza was antiseptically

raised, the servants' was not. Also note the difference between the balusters of the two. This interior may be the best illustration in this series of cruciform planning, expansion from a central core toward the four cardinal points, and, in this sense, is related to Wright's Willits house of 1902. This center, occupied by the stairway, was defined by the two axial fireplaces, the chimneys of which can be seen above the roof. Eight bedrooms and dressing chambers on the second floor and five on the third accommodated weekend and summer guests. The main floor included the basic rooms—hall (13′ × 18′) in oak, parlor (18′ × 24′) probably in pine, library (17′ × 20′) in California redwood and dining room (17′ × 20′) in cherry—but the smoking piazza and bay for plants were rare in these plans. A witty and flippant writer, popular lecturer and active architect in Boston, Walker (1857–1936) was the architect-in-chief of the Omaha Exposition of 1898 and the St. Louis Exposition of 1904.

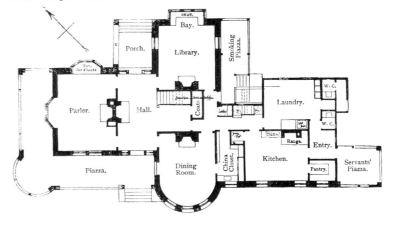

98. "Stonelea," George V. Cresson residence, Narragansett Pier, R.I.; McKim, Mead & White, architects, 1884. In 1894 the German art critic Wilhelm Bode observed that "the modern American house is built entirely from the inside outward and corresponds not only to the specific demands of the individual, but, above all, to particular American customs and requirements. That these are definitely and sharply stamped is the great advantage which the private architecture of the United States has over our German architecture." Applied to the plan of the Cresson house, this means that the smoking room was included because the owner wanted it, that the lavatory was included because its convenience overrode its social disadvantages, or that the dining room, hall and parlor could be compartmentalized or treated as one large space. In other words, Bode was saying that the particular steps requested by owners, or new arrangements reflecting social changes, or devices to increase comfort and convenience were valued above traditional practices and artistic conventions. To state this in yet another way, the hold of the grand tradition of architecture on American work of the late nineteenth century was shaky. Distinctiveness rather than coordination determined the finish of each of the main rooms of the Cresson plan. The hall was done in oak; the drawing room, more graceful, in white and gold; the dignity of the dining room was expressed in mahogany; and the den-like smoking room finished in cherry with cork sheathing on the walls. As Bode noted, these houses were often built from the inside outward, actually upward and outward from the hall. The shapes of the smoking room and the parlor express this centrifugal movement; however, the facade was seldom a direct reflection of the plan, as some Europeans contended. The Cresson house is a case in point. Here the principal section of the exterior is relatively contained and symmetrical while the plan tends to be outward

moving and asymmetrical. Furthermore, the character of the interior is dissimilar to that of the exterior. The organization of the former is contemporary, uncomplicated and efficient, quite representative of McKim, Mead & White in these years, but the exterior is not. The sliding board roof and Kaiser-helmeted dormers prove that architecture can be humorous. This aspect even attracted the eye of E. Eldon Deane, a popular sketcher for the *American Architect and Building News* (Nov. 21, 1885), who had a soft spot for the picturesque. "Stonelea" was built for $26,000 for George V. Cresson of Philadelphia, the president of a huge firm which he founded in 1859 to manufacture ropes, wheels, pulleys and drive shafts to transmit power. Though altered, the house still stands on its site on Newton Avenue.

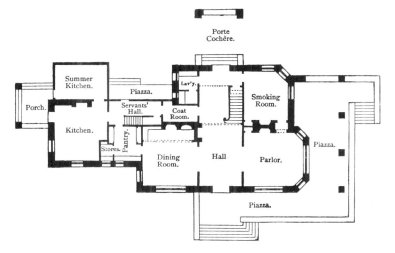

99. "Stoneleigh," H. S. Leech residence, Saratoga Springs, N.Y.; S. Gifford Slocum, architect, 1886. This summer house was built by Leech, a resident of New York City, in the years when Saratoga Springs was unrivaled as an island watering place. The exact date of the construction of "Stoneleigh" is unknown; the 1886 city directory was the first to indicate that the Leech family lived at this location. Erected on the southeast corner of Union Avenue and Circular Street, it was owned by the family until 1896. From 1897 until 1899 the house was vacant, suggesting that the demand for such large houses in Saratoga was waning or that potential buyers ridiculed its exuberant but ingenuous Queen Anne character. Purchased by Skidmore College in 1931 and converted into a dormitory, it was destroyed by fire in 1937. If this incredible exterior was representative of Slocum's design skill, we can understand why he is not better known today. He may have attended, but did not graduate from, Cornell University. He maintained an architectural office in Saratoga Springs, though not continuously, from 1882 until 1895. Handling the first story of Connecticut and New Jersey brownstone reasonably well, Slocum indulged his imagination above. The bay of the library, which began as a square form, ended four stories later as an octagonal one. The balconies paid tribute to numerous points on the compass. In fact, this house may have had more balconies than there were Leeches. These intermediate spaces—verandas, porches, balconies, etc.—which lay between the family's castle and the public world were important not only for informal living but also for reasons of health. Frightened by the increased talk about germs, high death rates from consumption and rising congestion and pollution in the cities, families used these spaces throughout the day and night. Although not as popular as it was to become just before the First

World War, the sleeping porch was common in the 1880s. Some of the balconies of the Leech house were probably used for this purpose, judging from their number and the solid walls around several of them. "Stoneleigh" was an odd name for a house primarily covered with shingles and half-timber work set between cement panels. The principal rooms were elegantly finished, the hall and dining room in antique quartered oak, the parlor in ebony, the sitting room in oak, and the library in mahogany with a high wainscot and a Lincrusta-Walton ceiling. Lincrusta-Walton, created in 1872 by Frederick Walton, an Englishman, was an easily washed decorative relief made of solidified linseed oil. "Lin" referred to linseed and "crusta" to relief.

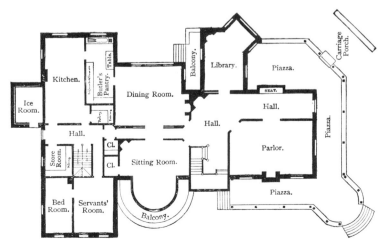

100. "Vinland," Louis L. Lorillard residence, Newport, R.I.; Peabody and Stearns, architects, 1884. Catherine Lorillard Wolfe was the original owner of this beautifully situated estate on Ochre Point, having commissioned the house in 1882. Approximately $200,000 were spent initially on the grounds, structure and furnishings. "The baptismal font on the south piazza is . . . a curiosity bought in Italy by Miss Wolfe's agent, who had *carte blanche* to secure for her whatever treasures of art or archaeology his judgment approved as suitable for the Newport villa, and who sometimes sent a contingent costing thirty thousand dollars." Subsequently owned by Louis L. Lorillard and enlarged by Peabody and Stearns in 1907, "Vinland" is extant. According to Wheaton Holden, it was designed in "no specific style" but is more "Romanesque in feel than in fact." The solidity of this brownstone villa and its size (168′ × 58′) verify that the summer domestic architecture at Newport was generally more substantial than at other leading resorts. A staff of six gardeners prepared the lawns and ornamental flower beds for the season. The grand sweep of the driveway and its drain system that minimized mud, the crisp edges of the smooth lawn, the carefully chosen and placed trees, the conspicuous souvenirs of antiquity effectively expressed control, order, means and good taste. The lawn of the ocean side was open, permitting the curious who strolled along the three-mile Cliff Walk to watch the Lorillards at play. Because a state law guaranteed public access to the shoreline, these millionaires had to endure lawful trespassers at the end of their backyards. However, their privacy was partially protected by a nineteenth-century American commodity—space. According to an impressed reporter for the Liverpool *Evening Standard* in 1896, "There is nothing to prevent you, if you are rude enough, from walking up the lawn and staring into Mr. Lorillard's, or any other cottager's lordly win-

dows. No one does, but anybody might. . . . The result is such a combination of natural and contrived beauty, open for the enjoyment of all, as is not to be seen on such terms anywhere else in the world." Sheldon was much impressed by this residence, calling it "one of the most comfortable, commodious, and beautiful country-seats in the world." He also appreciated its synthesis of new wealth and old culture. "The painful air of a plebian newness is missing. One thinks of the English manor-house, and its centuries of associations." Richard Codman of Boston, responsible for all interior decoration, installed a canvas frieze by the well-known English decorator Walter Crane in the dining room, figures after William Morris and Burne-Jones in the window of the landing, finished Lorillard's den in inlaid sycamore in an Italian style, hung the walls of the drawing room (35′ × 20′) with silk to achieve a Louis XVI air and draped the oak-beamed hall with Flemish tapestries.

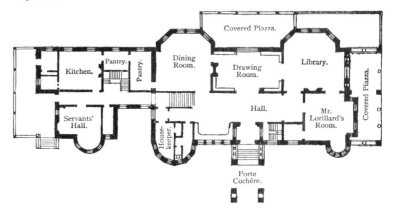